# Prayers for Southern People

*Poems and Prayers*
*for Christian Worship and Devotions*

# Joy Kingsbury-Aitken

Philip
Garside
Publishing Ltd.

Contact Joy at
email: jmk_dsa@hotmail.com

Paperback International edition 2023
ISBN  9781991027412

Also available
Paperback  New Zealand: ISBN 9781991027405
Paperback print-on-demand USA: ISBN 9798376459706
ePub: ISBN  9781991027436
PDF: ISBN  9781991027429

Philip Garside Publishing Ltd
PO Box 17160
Wellington 6147
New Zealand

books@pgpl.co.nz — www.philipgarsidebooks.com

Cover photo:
ID 182195442 © Victor Lapaev | Dreamstime
Two Peaks. Mount Cook and Mount Tasman.
Southern Alps, South Island, New Zealand

# Contents

# **Introduction**

Like *Prayers for Southern Seasons,* my first anthology of prayers and poems for Christian worship and devotions, this is a collection of prayers and poetic musings that have been written over several years for worship services I have taken or as an expression of my personal devotions, reflecting my engagement with scripture in the light of a wide range of contemporary issues.

*Prayers for Southern People* is divided into three sections. The first of these covers all the seasons in the church year as observed by churches following the *Revised Common Lectionary.* Thus readers will find in this section prayers and meditations relating to Advent, Christmas, Epiphany, Lent, Easter and Pentecost. For the Season of Pentecost I have adopted the Catholic tradition of calling this Ordinary Time, simply for ease of indexing. Thus the Day of Pentecost is clearly distinguishable from the Season of Pentecost.

The second section relates to the Season of Creation. This is a relatively new addition to the church year, endorsed ecumenically by Protestant, Anglican, Catholic and Orthodox churches. It lasts from 1 September, which is Creation Day in the Orthodox tradition, until 4 October, which in Catholicism is a memorial day for St Francis of Assisi, and is a day for blessing animals. The Season of Creation invites Christians to pray and act on behalf of our precious home the earth and all the wonderful species we humans share the earth with. As the impact of global warming intensifies, and the effects of human caused pollution becomes impossible to ignore, we are becoming increasingly aware of our God given mandate to take care of creation. This section contains prayers and meditations on all the environmental themes covered during the three year lectionary cycle, plus some extra themes recently added. The Hebrew Scriptures show that Israel's prophetic poets often invited creation to join with humanity in worshipping Israel's God. The Season of Creation invites us to rediscover this concept, and with it the idea that our relationship with creation was intended to be one of guardianship not exploitation.

The third section arises from my involvement with an environmental and social justice group within my home church. Some of the social issues reflected upon in this section have already been identified by the church as sufficiently important to have a Sunday assigned for their consideration, and are included in an "Additional Readings" section of the *Lectionary and Calendar* published jointly by the Methodist Church of New Zealand and the Presbyterian Church of Aotearoa/New Zealand. Others are included in the United Nations calendar of special days. Where two topics are closely aligned (e.g. trafficking in persons and modern slavery) these have been combined and could be the focus of a

Sunday in either of the specified months. This section provides humanitarian focused devotional and liturgical material. The church has identified appropriate special readings for the topics that have an assigned Sunday, and in the appendices I have suggested possible readings for the UN days.

Scriptures that informed my thinking are listed under the title of each prayer or meditative poem. The latter may prove suitable for the "devotions" item commencing the agendas of church meetings. Naturally I don't consider God gendered, but from time to time do use gendered language such as "Lord", the subversive title given to Jesus by the early church, as I expect my readers to discern the difference between metaphorical and literal language. I hope they will find within this anthology words to inspire and support their veneration of the divine and prayers that are useful for them when leading worship.

• • •

## Definitions

**Opening/Gathering:** Prayers for commencing worship, calls to worship.

**Candle lighting:** Prayers for the ritual of lighting of candles.

**Praise/Thanksgiving:** Prayers that praise God and give thanks for God's provision.

**Intercession:** Prayers for others, and for us in relation to others.

**Confession:** Prayers of contrition.

**Illumination:** Prayers for understanding the scriptures.

**Offering dedication:** Prayers dedicating gifts for the work of the church.

**Blessing:** Benedictions.

**Commissioning:** Concluding prayers, sending forth.

**Meditation:** Meditative poetry.

Prayers with lines in **bold** type can be read responsively.

# Part 1: The Liturgical Year

# *Advent*

## The Advent Candles (Candle lighting)

### The Hope Candle

The candles we light remind us
that Christ is the Light of the World.
The candles we light remind us
what it means to live in his light.
The First Advent candle we light
acclaims the blessing of hope.
The hope that comes from Jesus,
the founder of our hope.
The hope we have of resurrection
made possible by Jesus.
We light the candle for hope
in peace, with joy, and out of love. Amen.

### The Peace Candle

The candles we light remind us
that Christ is the Light of the World.
The candles we light remind us
what it means to live in his light.
The Second Advent candle we light
celebrates the blessing of peace.
The peace that comes from Jesus,
the prince of peace.
The peace of mind he gives us
irrespective of our circumstances.
We light the candle for peace in hope,
with joy, and out of love. Amen.

### The Joy Candle

The candles we light remind us
that Christ is the Light of the World.
The candles we light remind us
what it means to live in his light.
The Third Advent candle we light
expresses the blessing of joy.

The joy that comes from Jesus,
the source of our joy.
The life enhancing joy he gives
to all his faithful disciples.
We light the candle for joy,
with hope, in peace, and out of love. Amen.

## The Love Candle

The candles we light remind us
that Christ is the Light of the World.
The candles we light remind us
what it means to live in his light.
The Fourth Advent candle we light
rejoices in the blessing of love.
The love that comes from Jesus,
the loving saviour.
The love he gives out of his
abounding merciful grace.
We light the candle for love,
with hope, in peace, and out of joy. Amen.

## Remember (Intercession)

Remember all those travelling unwillingly at this season, O God,
especially refugees fleeing their homes,
that were once sanctuaries of peace and family togetherness,
but are now places of danger and fractured communities.
Remember them as you remembered Mary and Joseph
travelling south from Nazareth to Bethlehem,
and then fleeing as refugees from Bethlehem to Egypt.

Remember the lonely ones this season, O God,
especially those for whom Christmas is a reminder of
love lost, lives departed, liberty forfeited.
Come to the difficult folk who don't fit in,
the ones who break the rules,
the afflicted, the addicted, the dirty and despised.
Remember them as you remembered the lowly shepherds,
and sent your angels with tidings of great joy.

Remember the ones who need a home this season, O God,
young folk who haven't the resources to pay market rates for rents,
those who are camping out in garages and caravans
or couch sleeping in lounges where there are no bedrooms to spare,
longing for a place and a space of their own;
and children getting sick because of over-crowding.
Remember them as you remembered the needs of a baby boy
and sent the wise ones with valuable gifts.

Although inequality and iniquity persist,
love somehow survives,
and with it comes hope, joy and peace.
May all people everywhere experience these treasures,
your gifts to us this Christmas. Amen.

## Beginning a New Church Year (Intercession)

*Luke 1:46-55, 67-79; Matthew 6:10*

Lord we are beginning a new church year,
and approaching the end of another secular year,
knowing that there is still suffering in the world.
We see the evils of oppressive governments,
of conflict, of corruption, of exploitation,
and like the people in the days of
Elizabeth and Zechariah and Mary and Joseph,
we pray for the coming of your kingdom,
that your will be done on earth as it is in heaven.

Lord we are beginning a new church year,
and approaching the end of another secular year,
seeking hope for a better future for everyone,
seeking peace in place of wars and violent uprisings,
seeking out-going compassionate love to abolish the attitudes
that lead to conflict, corruption and exploitation,
and anticipating joy at the breaking in of your kingdom,
where things are done on earth as they are done in heaven. Amen.

## The Blessing of Peace (Blessing)

*Luke 2:14; John 14:27; Philippians 4:7*

May the peace the angels announced to the shepherds
be the peace you experience this season of Advent.
May the peace that Jesus gives to his disciples
be a precious gift you receive this Christmas.
May the peace of God that is beyond understanding
be yours throughout the year ahead.
May the blessings of God – Father, Son and Spirit –
fill you this summer with the peace
that accompanies hope, joy and love. Amen.

## Saying "Yes" to God (Commissioning)

*Luke 1:38; Philippians 4:6-7; John 14:27*

The story of the nativity begins with Mary saying "Yes" to God
in spite of the criticism that would surely come her way.
May you be as brave as Mary by also saying "Yes" to God
in spite of the scepticism that could possibly come your way.
God grant you a faith like Mary's and the fortitude to answer God's call.
God give you a hope like Mary's when God's plans for you are revealed.
Be joyful and go from here confidently with a mind that is at peace,
God's blessed gift given to you through Jesus, Mary's sacred son. Amen.

# *Christmas*

## The Christ Candle (Candle lighting)

*John 1:1-14; Isaiah 62:11-12*

In the middle of summer
when the sun is strongest
and daylight lasts longer than dark,
we still need the light
that comes from the Christ
that is stronger than sunlight,
with greater brilliance than diamonds
and more sparkle than a crystal chandelier.
For the light from the Christ
overcomes the darkness within,
by his indwelling presence
inspiring faith giving hope
and love giving peace.

In gratitude and with praise,
on this festive day
we light the Christ candle
as a symbol of the light
that has come into the world.
The light that began
when a baby was born,
that could not be extinguished
by the darkness of evil,
its radiance revealed
in the glory of resurrection.
We light the Christ candle
because the Saviour has come. Amen.

## The Wonder of Incarnation (Opening/Gathering)

*Colossians 1:17, 26-27; Luke 2:13-14*

Today we celebrate the wonder of incarnation.
The wonder that God's desire to dwell with us
took the form of a helpless human baby
born into a violent world to a peasant family.

Today we celebrate the joy of incarnation.
The joy that God has such a great love for us
as to be born as we are born, live as we live
and die a violent death that too many of us die.

Today we celebrate the hope of incarnation.
The hope of glory through Jesus Christ our Lord,
who became one of us to save every one of us
and to reconcile to God all things everywhere.

Today we celebrate the promise of incarnation.
The promise made through prophets and angels
that God plans for us to live in harmony so there
will be peace on earth for people of goodwill. Amen.

## Jesus, Where Were You Found? (Praise/Thanksgiving)

Jesus, where were you found?
Among the courtiers in Herod's gilded palace
or in a shelter where shepherds felt welcome?
Where were you found?
In a prince's ornate cradle in a royal nursery
or in a feeding trough in a rustic dwelling?
Where were you found?
Among the rich and powerful in the great city of Rome
or with the poor and oppressed in tiny Bethlehem?

Jesus, where can you be found?
In hill top mansions among the rich and famous
or down in the valleys with the poor in the slums?
Where can you be found?
Among those who slumber between sheets made of silk
or with the rough sleepers trying to survive on the streets?
Where can you be found?
Among narcissistic autocrats and their complicit enablers
or with desperate refugees fleeing from persecution?

Jesus, where are you to be found?
Beyond the stars and down here on earth?
In a heavenly temple and in a simple chapel?
Where are you to be found?
You are the Son at the right hand of the Father.
You are Emmanuel, you are God with us.
Where are you to be found?
You are wherever people gather in your name.
You are here among us as we celebrate your birth.

Jesus, where have you found us?
In both hovel and palace you come among us,
for human poverty or power are nothing to you.
You speak to everyone who is willing to listen,
and invite all to join you in the work that you do.
Your coming means more than an excuse for a party,
even though your coming is cause for great joy.
Your coming is a summons to a new way of living,
for the spirit of giving to continue all through the year. Amen.

## This Christmas (Blessing)

*John 1:4, 11; Matthew 2:2; Luke 2:14*

This Christmas may you be blessed
with a gift greater than any you will find
wrapped in colourful paper
and placed under an artificial tree.
This Christmas may you be blessed
with a radiance greater than any
string of LED Christmas lights
that flash and sparkle in the night.
This Christmas may you be blessed
with music greater than any
popular Christmas song
broadcast incessantly in December.
This Christmas may you be
illuminated by the light of Christ,
God's gift to humankind;
whose birth was marked by
a mysterious star and angels
singing, "Glory to God on high."

With them may you sing wholeheartedly
anthems of joyful praise,
because Christ has made it possible
for you to be a child of God. Amen.

### How Easy it is to Forget (Meditation)

*Luke 2:1-6; Matthew 2:13-18; Hebrews 9:25-28*

During the fun filled festivities of Christmas
how easy it is to forget
that this feast celebrates a birth
during a time of oppression and fear.

During the joyful gathering of families
how easy it is to forget
that a Roman census forced Joseph and Mary
to leave their home and those most dear.

During the pleasure of summer travel
how easy it is to forget
that the holy family became refugees
because of King Herod's murderous decree.

It's easy to remember at Christmas
the joy of the birth of a child,
but Christmas should also remind us
of the sin offering that child chose to be. Amen.

### Christmas in Summer (Meditation)

Christmas in summer means
strawberries and cream,
white Christmas lilies
and red pohutukawa blooms.
Christmas in summer means
juicy black cherries
and sweet boysenberries,
and sugary treats
like jelly and ice cream.
Christmas in summer means
picnics and barbeques,
fun filled gatherings
with family and friends.

Christmas in summer
means hiking and biking,
celebrating incarnation
in the great outdoors.
Christmas in summer
is a season of joyfulness,
when the generosity of the earth
shows the graciousness of God.
Christmas in summer
is not a day but a season
of joyful praise and
prayerful thankfulness
for the wonders of creation
and the gifts of life.
For under the warm summer sun
of a down-under Christmas
we remember the gospel begins
with the hope and the joy that
accompanies a birth.

## In the beginning, the Word (Meditation)
*John 1:1-3, 14; Genesis 1:31, 3:6; Hebrews 5:8*

In the beginning, the Word
was with God and was God.
The Word spoke,
and with a rush and a roar
the universe came into being.
Stars formed, galaxies spiralled
and planets orbited their suns.
Everything came into being
through the Word that spoke;
and God saw that what
had come into being was good.

In the beginning, the Word
was with God and was God.
The Word spoke,
and life began on a small planet
circling a minor star on the edge
of an unexceptional galaxy.
Lush vegetation covered the earth
where great beasts roamed,
and in its restless oceans
huge sea creatures swam;
and God saw that what
had come into being was good.

In the beginning, the Word
was with God and was God.
The Word spoke,
and a new kind of creature emerged.
One who asked questions
and sought understanding,
who in acquiring knowledge
also stumbled into evil.
One whose sense of the divine
led to a need to be worshipful.
One with whom the Word could talk;
and God saw that what
had come into being was good.

In the beginning, the Word
was with God and was God.
The Word spoke
from the top of a mountain
to a refugee people
traversing a harsh wilderness,
giving them principles to live by
when they became a new nation
in a land the Word
had promised to Abraham;
and God saw that what
had come into being was good.

In the beginning, the Word
was with God and was God.
The Word spoke
through storytellers and singers,
poets and prophets,
inspiring a holy book,
telling the story of a people
striving and failing
to comprehend God and live
as the Word instructed;
and God saw that what
had come into being was good.

In the beginning, the Word
was with God and was God.
The Word spoke
to his own people
who did not accept him,
when as a man he was born
among a people oppressed.
Through suffering he learnt
what it means to obey;
and God saw that what
had come into being was good.

In the beginning, the Word
was with God and was God.
The Word spoke
in parables and proverbs
teaching disciples,
who established a church
to spread the good news
that his reign on earth has begun.
In worship we honour the Word
who made flesh lived among us;
and God sees that what
is coming into being
will be very good. Amen.

# *New Year*

**New Year's Eve** (Praise/Thanksgiving)

Day by day, hour by hour this year has passed
leaving only memories
of moments of joy
and times of sorrow,
of times when we have laughed heartily
and of times when we have silently shed tears.

Day by day, hour by hour this year has passed
leaving only memories
of happy family gatherings
and times of sweet solitude,
of occasions full of busyness
and times of restful idleness.

Day by day, hour by hour this year has passed
during which we have experienced your grace,
through the bounty of the earth,
in the beauty of living things,
in the warmth of heavenly sunshine
and the cool of refreshing rain.

Day by day, hour by hour this year has passed
and now on the eve of a new year
we give thanks for your loving presence
which we have experienced throughout
the year that's been.

We give thanks for the year now gone
and anticipate the year now coming,
knowing the blessing of your company,
in good times and in bad,
when we're happy and when we're sad. Amen

## **This Year Ahead** (Intercession)

*Mark 1:15*

The triumphs and tragedies
of the year just behind us
throw light and cast shadows
over the year ahead of us.
We know that hanging up
a new calendar changes little.

Yet in wishing one another
a "happy new year"
we are expressing our
collective hope that this year
we will all experience the blessings
that really matter:
Loving relationships
good health
secure and warm homes
plentiful and nourishing food
meaningful work, and
opportunities for fun.

Fireworks that flash and bang in the night
noisy parties that go on far too long
disturbing the neighbourhood,
resolutions quietly abandoned
before good habits are formed;
such are the traditions with which
we mark the start of a new year.

If only we were celebrating the end of:
hunger and homelessness
greed and corruption
exploitation and war
pollution and disease,
rather than just the passing of time.

Every year we feel overwhelmed
by the problems confronting humanity.
Every year we feel disempowered
by our inability as individuals
to make a big difference.
Every year we pray, "your kingdom come,
your will be done on earth as it is in heaven."

This year, even if conflicts destroy
lives and livelihoods,
even if extreme weather events
gather momentum,
and even if multitudes suffer
from famine and disease,
we will again affirm that we believe
the time is fulfilled,
that the kingdom of God draws near.

We hear your call to repent, to change direction,
and we respond by asking that this year God you
inspire, encourage and help humanity
to do what is needed to bring about a reduction in
hunger and homelessness
greed and corruption
exploitation and war
pollution and disease.

This year, inspire, encourage
and help us your church
to feed the hungry
and shelter the impoverished,
to cry out against the oppression
of the weak and vulnerable,
to champion justice and promote peace,
and to work at healing the earth and its people. Amen.

## New Year's Blessing (Blessing)

*Galatians 5:22*

God bless you throughout the year ahead
with joy unrestrained regardless of loss,
with peace untroubled by the presence of problems,
with courage unconquered by the causes of fear,
with patience unaffected by hope being delayed,
with kindness uninhibited by the indifference of others,
with generosity unconstrained by another's selfishness,
with faithfulness unshakeable by life's uncertainties,
with gentleness unchecked by the world's callousness,
with restraint untroubled by alluring temptations,
and with an unending love for God and for people.
God bless you with the fruit of the Spirit this year. Amen.

# *Epiphany*

## Like the Magi Who Saw a Star (Opening/Gathering)

*Matthew 2:1-12; John 1:9; Mark 1:1-8; Luke 2:22-38; Isaiah 49:6-7*

Like the magi who saw a star as a sign of the birth of a king
and travelled from the east to pay homage to him,
**we see the true light that enlightens everyone
and have come together today to worship him.**

Like the crowds who flocked to the Jordan River
to hear and be baptised by the prophet John
**we congregate to venerate the One John proclaimed
would baptise the faithful with the Holy Spirit.**

Like Simeon and Anna who welcomed the Christ child
when he was brought to the temple for his presentation
**we welcome the Messiah among us this morning
our Lord, the Redeemer, the Holy One. Amen.**

## Guided by the Gospels (Illumination)

*Matthew 2:1-12*

Like the magi were guided by a star to the holy Christ Child,
may we be guided by the gospels to comprehend Jesus better.
Like the magi brought with them gold, frankincense and myrrh,
may we bring with us an enquiring mind and a faithful heart.
Like the magi who knelt before Jesus to pay him homage,
may the scriptures inspire and enhance our worship of God. Amen.

## Like the Magi who Brought You Gold (Offering Dedication)

*Matthew 2:11; Revelation 8:3-4*

Like the magi who brought you gold
we give you some of our resources
for the work of your church.

Like the magi who brought you frankincense
we offer up prayers to you
for the blessing of your church.

Like the magi who brought you myrrh
we support the preaching of the gospel
for the well-being of your church.

May our gifts of treasure and time
be used by you to bring hope and healing
to the world beyond the walls of your church. Amen.

## The Season of Epiphany is For Us a Summer Season (Intercession)

The season of Epiphany is for us a summer season;
a time for travelling to new and exciting places,
a time for holidaying with family and friends.
The season of Epiphany is for us a refreshing season;
a time for going to the beach and the bush,
a time for recharging our bodies and refreshing our minds.
The season of Epiphany is for us an in-between season;
a time for celebrating what has been achieved,
a time for anticipating what is yet to come.
The season of Epiphany is a grace-filled season.
**With the magi the church once again traverses deserts
to encounter the Christ and bring others to Him.**

God be with all who are travelling this summer.
Keep them safe on our roads, in the sea and the sky.
God bless all families who are together this summer
and comfort those who are far apart from loved ones.
God bless all who seek relaxation and rejuvenation this summer
and bless all who are working this holiday season.
God bless all who are happy and joyful this summer
and lift up all who are burdened with worries and fears.
**With the magi the church once again traverses deserts
to encounter the Christ and bring others to Him.**

God you are with us in all our circumstances this season.
We thank you for the times when the living is easy.
We thank you for your presence when the living is hard.
God before Epiphany in summer comes around again,
during the autumn and winter and spring seasons of life,
help us to become more attuned to your thinking,
help us live lives more aligned with your serving.
God before Epiphany in summer comes around again, may
**with the magi the church again traverse deserts
and encounter the Christ and bring others to him. Amen.**

## Christ Give Us (Intercession)

*Matthew 2:1-12; John 1:29-34; 1 Samuel 3:9-10; Mark 1:16-20, 29.*

Christ give us the eyes we need
to see your signs that summon us,
so that we may be like the magi who
were beckoned by a star to pay homage to you.
Christ give us the voice we need
to testify to the truth of you,
so that we may be like the Baptiser who
proclaimed you to be the Lamb of God.
Christ give us the ears we need
to hear you when you are calling us,
so that we may be like Samuel who
said, "Speak Lord, your servant is listening."
Christ give us the feet we need
to step out in faith and follow you,
so that we may be like the disciples who
left their work to learn from you.
Christ give us the hands we need
to attend to those who require our help,
so that we may be like Peter's mother-in-law who
after being healed ministered to you. Amen.

## Epiphany Blessing (Blessing)

*Matthew 2:1-2; John 1:29-34, 2:3-9*

During your day to day life
may you be guided by the Christ
like his star guided the Magi
in their quest to pay him homage.
During your day to day life
may you be identified as a child of God
like John the Baptist recognised Jesus
as the Lamb of God, the Saviour.
During your day to day life
may you perceive God's abundant blessings
like the guests who enjoyed the best wine
towards the end of the wedding feast at Cana.
During this season of Epiphany
may you grow in faithfulness and love
by being coached, approved and cherished
by the faithful God of love. Amen.

## The Baptism of Jesus (Meditation)

*Mark 1:9-11, 14-15; Luke 3:15-16; John 13:34-35*

Immersion in the living waters of the Jordan
under the supervision of the Baptiser John
marked the beginning of something new,
a transition point in the life of this Jew.

No longer would he labour as a carpenter,
but rather as a prophet he would proclaim
that the time had come to repent and believe
the good news of the nearness of God's reign.

What began in Bethany across the Jordon
became inevitable in Bethany outside Jerusalem,
when Mary anointed Jesus as her Messiah
not truly understanding the nature of his mission.

Having made enemies among the powerful,
the local collaborators with the foreign occupiers,
this man would not sit upon a golden throne
but be nailed to the wood of a Roman cross.

John the Baptiser had proclaimed that Jesus was
the Lamb of God who takes away the world's sin,
and the voice of God declared at his baptism,
"You are my beloved Son; with you I am well pleased."

He emerged from the cold waters of the Jordan
just as he would emerge from the cold of the tomb,
and the dove that descended on him at his baptism
is the Holy Spirit he now immerses the faithful in.

So on this day when we commemorate the baptism
of Jesus, our Lord and Saviour, the eternal Christ,
let us prove ourselves worthy to be his disciples
by loving others as greatly as he showed he loves us. Amen.

# *Transfiguration*

**Listen to him** (Praise/Thanksgiving)

*Matthew 17:5; Exodus 3:2-12, 23:20-22; 1 Kings 19:11-13*

"This is my dearly beloved son, who brings me great joy.
Listen to him."

He is the mighty messenger
who appeared to the shepherd Moses
in the blazing fire of a bush not consumed.
"I am the God of Abraham, Isaac and Jacob," he said.
"I will send you to Pharaoh to bring my people out of Egypt."
First Moses objected, then listened, then led a people to freedom.
**"This is my dearly beloved son, who brings me great joy.**
**Listen to him," the voice of God said.**

He is the mighty messenger
who in a pillar of cloud and fire stood between Israelites and Egyptians
while the wind of the Lord blew a path through the sea.
He is the angel God sent before them guarding them on their way.
"Listen attentively to his voice and do all that I say," said God,
"then I will be an enemy to your enemies, and a foe to your foes."
**"This is my dearly beloved son, who brings me great joy.**
**Listen to him," the voice of God said.**

He is the soundless messenger
who the prophet Elijah could not hear
in the howling hurricane, the crashing earthquake,
and the roaring of a raging fire.
For God speaks as a sound of sheer silence.
This Elijah heard, he listened and obeyed.
**"This is my dearly beloved son, who brings me great joy.**
**Listen to him," the voice of God said.**

He is the humble messenger of good news
the incarnate One who appeared in all his glory
to frightened followers on a hilltop in Galilee.
In a vision they saw him speaking with Moses and Elijah.
**"This is my dearly beloved son, who brings me great joy.**
**Listen to him," the voice of God said.**

This is the servant messenger who died for us and lives for us
Jesus the Messiah, who calls us to follow him
and to love each other as he loves each of us.
God speaks to us through his words spoken to the disciples.
**"This is my dearly beloved son, who brings me great joy.
Listen to him," the voice of God said. Amen.**

## Stories like these (Illumination)

There are times when the impenetrable boundary
between heaven and earth appears to have been crossed,
and mortals were given a brief glimpse of the divine.
The event we call the Transfiguration of Christ
was just such an extraordinary occurrence.
God when we encounter stories like these
that are remote from our everyday experiences,
help us comprehend them at a far deeper level
than the facts of what happened and to whom. Amen.

## Send down on Others and Us Your Glorious Grace (Intercession)

*Matthew 17:1-9; 2 Kings 2:1-13; Exodus 34:29-35;
2 Corinthians 3:12 – 4:6*

Christ whose glory your disciples temporarily glimpsed
on the summit of the Mount of Transfiguration,
send down on others and us your glorious grace,
especially when we're caught up in a whirlwind of grief.
Come to us majestically as in a chariot of fire
and sweep us all up into your loving presence.
May those who are exhausted with worry and work
have someone to pass their mantle on to.

God whose glory manifested itself as a swirling cloud
on the summit of the Mount of Transfiguration,
send down on others and us your glorious grace,
especially when we're cloaked in clouds of fear.
Come to us gently as a voice of encouragement
and invite us all into your loving presence.
May those feeling smothered by their many troubles
see their burdens disappear like dissolving mist.

Holy Spirit whose glory was proclaimed by
the lawgiver Moses and the prophet Elijah,
send down on others and us your glorious grace,
especially when we're oblivious to your truth.

Come to us brilliantly as divine revelation
and draw us all into your loving presence.
May those who cannot see your truth clearly
have the veil over their minds lifted by you.

God whose glory is beyond human comprehension
and whose love for us is greater than we can perceive,
hear our prayer for others and for ourselves;
our request that you comfort those who grieve,
our request that you reassure those who worry,
our request that you convince those who doubt,
and that all your people will be encouraged
by their experience of you and your glorious grace. Amen.

## His Power and Majesty (Blessing)

May the Christ who gave his disciples an impression of his glory
when they were with him on the Mount of Transfiguration,
also give you insight into his power and majesty,
that will inspire you during your hill top experiences
and encourage you when you are down in the valleys.
May the God who is Creator, Christ and Comforter bless you
by accompanying you throughout the adventure that is your life. Amen.

## Followers of the Glorified Christ (Commissioning)

*Revelation 1:12-15; Mark 9:2-8; Philippians 2:6-8; Hebrews 4:12;
John 1:1-3, 14*

You are followers of the glorified Christ.
The holy one whose face is dazzling bright
like the summer sun shining at high noon,
and whose garments glisten like
the light reflected off purest snow,
white beyond human ability to bleach.
The one whose feet gleam like burnished brass
and whose eyes are aflame with the fire of righteousness.

You are followers of the glorified Christ.
The holy one who set aside his splendour
and emptied himself of his power
to be incarnated as a humble human,
so that he might redeem his own creation
from the corruption of our sinfulness,
through his obedience to the point
of suffering and dying on the cross.

You are followers of the glorified Christ.
The holy one whose words cut through
our duplicity with the efficacy of a two-edged sword.
He's the Father's beloved Son, the Word
whom God commands we pay attention to.
So go out from here listening for his voice
in the stirrings of your heart through the
scriptures you read, and the wisdom you hear spoken. Amen.

## The Cloud of Your Glory (Meditation)

*Luke 9:34-35, 21:27; Exodus 40:34-38; 1 Kings 8:10-11; Daniel 7:13-14;*
*Acts 1:6-11; Revelation 1:7, 14:14*

God on the day that Jesus was transfigured,
your word speaks of the disciples being terrified
by the cloud that descended upon them.
Had this been an ordinary water laden cloud
they may have felt cold and damp but not afraid.
But this was the cloud of your glory
imbued with your immense mystical power.

God your word speaks of a cloud descending
upon the tent of meeting in the wilderness.
Even your servant Moses was kept from entering
the tabernacle by the power of your glory,
filling the tent of meeting night and day,
where it stayed until it was time for the Israelites
to set out on the next stage of their journey.

God your word tells us that at the dedication
of the temple Solomon had built in Jerusalem,
the cloud of your glory filled the holy place
preventing the priests from ministering inside.
In exile Daniel had a vision of a divine being
like a Son of Man coming with the clouds of heaven
to receive dominion and glory from the Ancient of Days.

God this was the cloud into which the Risen Christ
ascended on the day he was taken into heaven.
This is the cloud in which the Son of Man comes
with power and great glory back to the earth.
God your word speaks of the cloud of your glory
from the Torah to the Book of Revelation,
for the cloud of your glory signifies your holiness.

# *Lent*

## Lighting a Candle during Lent (Candle lighting)

*Isaiah 58:6-7; Luke 4:17-21*

We light a candle during Lent for all who are imprisoned unjustly.
**We remember that Jesus was robbed of his liberty and his life.**

We light a candle during Lent for all who are in some form of bondage.
**We remember that Jesus came to set the captives free.**

We light a candle during Lent for all who are hungry and homeless.
**We remember that Jesus depended on others for food and shelter.**

We light a candle during Lent for all who suffer.
**We remember that by his suffering on the cross Jesus was glorified, and that by alleviating the suffering of others we share in his glory. Amen.**

## We begin Lent (Opening/Gathering)

On this Ash Wednesday…
We begin Lent by remembering our Messiah.
The Son of Man who was the Son of God,
who divested of glory became one of us.

We begin Lent by remembering our origins.
From star dust the earth was formed
and we came forth out of the earth.

We begin Lent by remembering our end.
From dirt we came and to dirt we will return,
our bodies a gift of and a gift to the universe.

We begin Lent by remembering our limitations.
Our intellectual abilities and our technologies
are both enriching us and destroying us.

We begin Lent by remembering our waywardness.
Our regrets for what we have done and failed to do,
moving us to repentance and reconciliation.

We begin Lent by remembering our Saviour.
The Holy One who restores our bonds with God
and offers us new life through resurrection.

We begin Lent by remembering our frailty.
With humility we marvel that we earth creatures,
though sinful can yet become children of God.

We begin Lent by remembering our indebtedness.
With gratitude we thank the Triune God for forgiveness,
and for the gift of life now and in the age to come. Amen.

**The Season of Lent** (Praise/Thanksgiving)
*Matthew 5:48; Romans 5:10; Ephesians 2:4-5*
Lord Jesus Christ, from ages past the Season of Lent
has been a season for self-reflection,
**for acknowledging that we have not come**
**even close to the perfection you desire.**

Lord Jesus Christ, from ages past the Season of Lent
has been a season for deep appreciation
**of your willingness to forgive our iniquities,**
**and of our total dependence upon your grace.**

Lord Jesus Christ, from ages past the Season of Lent
has been a season for reconciliation,
**for healing any relationships we have broken,**
**for being grateful that you reconcile us to God.**

Lord Jesus Christ, from ages past the Season of Lent
has been a season of spiritual preparation,
**for focussing on the coming Holy Week**
**when your passion and resurrection will be recalled.**

Lord Jesus Christ, from ages past the Season of Lent
has been a season of renewed dedication
**to our calling as your disciples in this generation,**
**in response to your saving love and mercy. Amen.**

### Not By Bread Alone (Illumination)

*Deuteronomy 8:3; Luke 4:4*

Going without in Lent helps to remind us
that humanity does not live by bread alone
but needs the words that come from God.
Just as our bodies require regular feeding
so the spirit within us desires to be fed.
God nourish us today with the bread of learning
and give us the water of wisdom to drink.
Help our minds to be fully receptive
to the eternal truths that are contained
within the Scriptures about to be read. Amen.

### "Is not this the fast that I choose?" (Intercession)

*Isaiah 58:6-11; Luke 4:18*

God you inspired the prophet to write:
**"Is not this the fast that I choose:**
**to loosen the bonds of injustice…**
**to let the oppressed go free?"**

God we cry out for those suffering injustice,
those falsely accused and wrongly convicted.
Send champions to argue their case,
bring truth to light that they may go free.

God we cry out for those suffering imprisonment
for their political ideas or their religious beliefs.
Replace corrupt dictators with honest leaders
who will let the prisoners of conscience go free.

God you inspired the prophet to write:
**"Is not this the fast that I choose…**
**To share your bread with the hungry,**
**to bring the homeless poor into your house?"**

God we cry out for those suffering hunger,
those starving because of famine and war.
Let us who are rich give generously to the poor
while addressing the causes of climate change and conflict.

God we cry out for those without shelter,
the rough sleepers forced to dwell on the streets.
Help us provide sufficient warm and safe houses
for all folk to have a good place to call home.

God you inspired the prophet to write:
**"If you offer your food to the hungry**
**and satisfy the needs of the afflicted**
**then your light shall arise in the darkness and…**
**the LORD will guide you continually."**

God this Lent we remember that Jesus came
bringing good news to the poor,
proclaiming release to the captives
and freedom for all who are oppressed.

God this Lent grant to us a heart of compassion like Jesus
and show us how to bring prosperity to the impoverished,
obtain justice and liberation for the unlawfully imprisoned,
and provide comfort and aid to the afflicted and oppressed.

God may our fasting this Lent be the fasting you desire
of our actions being a blessing for all we encounter.
May our fasting this Lent lead to radical self-giving;
God guide us into living the way Jesus taught. Amen.

## Lenten Blessing (Blessing)

At a time when food is plentiful
we speak of a time of fasting,
for here in the southern hemisphere
Lent comes at the time of harvest.
Fast from the hurtful and spiteful
and gather in the fruits of kindness.
Fast from the mean and selfish
and gather in the fruits of generosity.
Fast from conflict and quarrels
and gather in the fruits of peace.
Fast throughout Lent in this way,
and experience the blessing of God. Amen.

## This Lent (Commissioning)

This Lent,
as once more you retrace,
the footsteps of Jesus,
from Galilee to Golgotha,
from acclamation to the cross,
remember that this is a story telling
how darkness was overwhelmed by light,
how death was overcome by resurrection.
The sparks of new life were ignited
when Jesus rose that first Easter morning.
A new world has begun evolving,
a new way of being has become possible.
So during your Lenten journey of self-reflection
and repentance for old world ways of living,
know that your failures are forgiven
and can't keep you from being
included in God's new creation story.
Be joyful, and give grateful thanks
for your access to the risen Jesus,
who is for you the Tree of Life. Amen.

## Treasures in Heaven (Meditation)

*Matthew 5:6, 6:19-21; 1 Corinthians 6:20*

Too often we judge our value according to the wealth we possess,
the worth of our share portfolio and how quickly our bank balance grows.
Does the size of the house we live in, and the price we paid for our clothes,
give even a slight indication of how much we as humans are worth?
Are we not far more valuable to God than the sum of the things we
possess?

The condition of our hearts is revealed by whatever it is we treasure,
and whether we focus on God or fix our eyes on the symbols of success.
The purpose of our Lenten fast is to become hungry for righteousness,
and to store up for ourselves in heaven the wealth that truly lasts;
for in Lent we recall how God paid a price beyond measure for us.

**The Season of Autumn** (Meditation)

The season of autumn is upon us.
Summer's warmth is past and winter's chill approaches.
Autumn flowering bulbs like crocus and nerines
give a final burst of colour before the greyness sets in.

The season of autumn is upon us.
A season for reaping the last of the harvest.
A season for planting in anticipation
of the colour and life that bursts forth in the spring.

The church in the west is in a season like autumn.
The fruits of the past are now all gathered in.
The faithful still gather but in numbers declining.
The dying of winter seems not far away.

God you are the gardener, we only the labourers
in your church as it prepares for the seasons ahead.
We need you to show us what needs to be planted,
where we should mulch and what prune away.

God you are the gardener, we only the labourers.
By our own efforts we can't grow your church,
but by our attitudes we can hamper its thriving,
our actions and dogmas can turn people away.

The church in the west is in a season like autumn,
but how things are now are not how they need be.
Proclaim through us God your life-giving gospel
to a new generation in a life-granting way. Amen.

# *Palm Sunday*

## Like Palm Waving Pilgrims (Opening/Gathering)

*John 12:12-19; Zechariah 9:9*

Like the palm waving pilgrims who escorted Jesus
down the Mount of Olives and into the temple in Jerusalem
**we too shout Hosanna to one who comes to save us.**

Like the Jerusalemites who came out of the city to greet their Messiah
**we too welcome the one who comes in the name of the Lord.**

Like the people who rejoiced greatly at the coming of their king,
righteous and humble, riding on a donkey
**we too acknowledge our allegiance to him who was
not installed on David's throne but nailed to a Roman cross. Amen.**

## A Broken and a Breaking People (Confession)

*Psalm 27:14, 118:25-26; John 12:13; Acts 1:6; Hebrews 5:8; Luke 22:43;
James 1:3*

Like the crowd that shouted, "Hosanna, save us now,"
at Jesus as he rode down the slopes of the Mount of Olives,
we too tend to shout at you God, save us from our troubles now.
We want quick fixes, we want to avoid suffering,
we want Easter Sunday without Good Friday coming first.

We live in a damaged world, a world largely broken by us.
We want to avoid the consequences of our actions,
the pain that arises when self-interest goes unchecked.
We look to you God to solve our problems for us.
We want blessings without repentance coming first.

Like the crowd that proclaimed Jesus to be their king,
like the disciples who hoped he was about to restore Israel,
like the believers who thought he'd return in their lifetime,
we want your programme God to adhere to our timetable.
We want your intervention in our troubles right now,
we don't want to wait for a future liberation.

If Jesus learned obedience through suffering, we do too,
and God you strengthen us in times of crisis as you did your Son.
We wait on you for deliverance, and this requires courage,
and while the testing of our faith produces endurance,
we confess to often feeling tired and impatient,
and to being discouraged and sometimes disillusioned.

God we confess that many of our problems are of our own making,
and acknowledge that it's up to us to implement their solutions.
Though you are always with us you don't indulgently clean up after us.
We are a broken and a breaking people, forgive us and transform us,
and during this holy season help us begin mending
what we have deeply hurt and greatly harmed. Amen.

## We Read Again (Illumination)

God, at this time of year we read again and reflect upon
familiar scriptures narrating the events of Holy Week.
This year help us examine these stories from a fresh perspective.
This year lead us to apply anew their lessons for our lives.
This year bring the Passion narratives into clearer focus,
as once more with singing psalms and waving palms
we welcome the one who comes in the name of the Lord. Amen.

## Anointed One who Gave Your All for Us (Offering Dedication)

*Mark 11:9-10, John 8:36, 18:36*

Anointed One who gave your all for us,
please accept from us the little we can give to you.
Redeemer One to whom the people cried Hosanna,
please accept from us these freewill offerings
in gratitude for the salvation we have through you.
Sovereign One who told the Roman Governor
your kingdom is not from this world,
please accept from us these gifts
for the growth of your kingdom in this world. Amen.

## The Peacemaker Messiah (Intercession)

*John 12:12-15; Isaiah 2:4*

A people whose land was being occupied by a colonising super-power,
a people living in poverty in spite of labouring long and hard,
a people oppressed by a wealthy elite who despised and exploited them,
these in the main were the people who proclaimed Jesus to be their King.

Nothing much has changed in the intervening two thousand years.
Ancestral lands are still being utilised and even stolen by alien occupiers.
Workers, now deemed to be essential, are still being inadequately paid,
and the exploited, impoverished and dispossessed still need a champion.

Jesus you were not the Messiah the palm wavers envisaged you would be –
someone to lead them in a violent uprising against their Roman overloads.
Rather Jesus you are the peacemaker Messiah who has eternity in view,
inspiring people everywhere in every age to beat swords into ploughshares.

Jesus you see the people suffering injustice, help us see them too.
Help us advocate for restoration and restitution
so they may be made whole.
Jesus you see the people being exploited, help us see them too.
Help us insist they be paid fairly and work safely
so they may be made whole.

Jesus you uphold the peacemakers, the justice seekers,
the boundary crossers,
the people righting wrongs, binding wounds, forming bonds,
creating accord.
Jesus may you include us in their number. May we be among the people
you inspire everywhere in every age to beat swords into ploughshares.
Amen.

## The Children of Israel came Shouting (Blessing)

The Children of Israel came shouting
"Hosanna" – Save us now.
The Children of God come singing
"Hallelujah" – God has saved us now.
Go through Holy Week solemnly
recalling the suffering of Jesus.
Go through Holy Week joyfully
remembering that Jesus was raised.
Go from here gratefully praising
God for his love, mercy and grace.
Go from here sure of God's blessing
on you and on all whom you love. Amen.

## As You Go into this Solemn Week (Commissioning)

During Lent we have been preparing
for these last few days of awe.
Holy Week has begun and we remember
that following the hope of this day
comes the day that tells a story of
betrayal, injustice, cruelty and death.

As you go out into this solemn week,
go knowing that the story
doesn't end with hope denied,
with the forces of evil triumphant.
Out of death has come new life,
through resurrection a new way of being.

Go from here rejoicing in being a blessed people,
for whom a new world has begun,
for whom the Kingdom of God has come.
Go from here living and spreading the good news
that God heard the people shout Hosanna
and through his Son is bringing salvation. Amen.

# *Maundy Thursday*

## We are in Need of Cleansing (Confession)

*John: 13:1-17; Matthew 7:13-14*

We are in need of cleansing.
Our feet are muddy from the paths we have trod.
Not the physical roads we travel along,
our feet protected by robust footwear,
but the pathways of our thoughts and actions,
where the potholes of self-centredness abound
and we too easily stumble into their muddy mire.

We are in need of cleansing.
Our life journey is towards the kingdom of God
along a difficult pathway that is hard to find.
Oftentimes we choose the wide, popular road,
the easy way, contaminated by selfishness,
rather than stick to the straight and narrow path,
the demanding way of self-giving love.

We are in need of cleansing.
Jesus you washed the feet of your disciples
the night of your betrayal and arrest.
Jesus we too are disciples with feet made dirty
from having walked in ways apart from you.
Jesus each year you rewash our feet by the hands
of those who serve both us and you. Amen.

## The Winegrower and the Vine (Blessing)

*John 4:14, 7:37-39, 15:1-11*

May you be greatly blessed
by the Winegrower who prunes
the fruit-bearing branches
to make them more productive.

May you be greatly blessed
by the Vine who sustains the branches.
He will cause you to bear much fruit
as long as you remain grafted into him.

May you be greatly blessed
by the Living Water who flows
through the Vine into the branches,
producing the juice that makes the finest wine.

May the joy of the Winegrower,
the Vine and Holy Spirit, abide in you,
and may your joy be complete. Amen.

## Not Realising (Meditation)

*Luke 22:14-27; 1 Corinthians 11:23-26; Matthew 26:30, 36-49;
Hebrews 2:15*

Jesus, not realising that they would not again
eat together in your physical company,
your disciples squabbled over whom among them
was to be regarded as the greatest,
so you demonstrated servant leadership
by humbly washing their dirty feet.
The first in our world comes last in your realm,
the one who serves is greater than the served.

Jesus, when the supper was concluded you broke bread,
and when distributing the pieces to your disciples you said,
"This is my body broken for you. Do this in remembrance of me."
Then you passed around a cup of wine, saying
"This is my blood of the covenant, poured out for many."
You achieved the goal of the law and the prophets,
for the giving of your life sealed the covenant
which God makes with all who believe in you.

Jesus, before leaving the upper room that night
you and your disciples sang a psalm together;
the Great Hallel which recalls how on Passover
God rescued the Israelites from Egyptian bondage.
Your disciples sang about the freeing of their people
not realising the deliverance you were about to achieve.
We remember how you liberated us on this Passover
not from tyrannical rulers but from the tyranny of death.

Jesus, not realising that you were about to be arrested
your disciples fell asleep while you fervently prayed,
seeking deliverance from the suffering you knew was coming
but bending your will to God's will nevertheless.
Then the betrayer arrived accompanied by soldiers.
Judas came to you and identified you with a kiss.
The world arraigned you that night and the next morning
not realising that it wasn't you but the world that was on trial.

# *Good Friday*

**A Day of Darkness** (Opening/Gathering)

A day of darkness
**yet the light was not overcome.**

A day of fearfulness
**yet immense courage was shown.**

A day of betrayal
**with unshakeable faithfulness on display.**

A day of hatred and death
**by which love and life were revealed.**

A day of disaster and evil,
**a day forever called "good."**

**Holy God, Compassionate and Merciful** (Praise/Confession)

*Mark 14 & 15, John 8:31-32, 18 & 19, Matthew 6:24, 7:2;
Luke 12:9, 14:27; Galatians 6:7; Romans 5:8, 6:6; Isaiah 53:5;
1 John 1:9; Ephesians 2:8*

Holy God, Compassionate and Merciful,
today is a day of remembrance.
A memorial day on which we recall that for us Jesus suffered
being betrayed by a disciple for thirty pieces of silver;
being denied by a friend whose courage deserted him;
being falsely accused by the chief priests' lackeys;
being found innocent yet condemned by a corrupt judge;
being mocked and cruelly scourged by heartless soldiers;
being forced to drag his cross through the city streets;
being stripped of his clothes and crucified.
**For us Jesus endured these things.**

Holy God, Compassionate and Merciful,
today is a day of remembrance.
A memorial day on which we recall that Jesus taught that
if we allow seeking wealth to be our master we cannot also serve God;
if we deny him before others he will deny us before the angels of God;
if we are to know the truth we must continue in his word;
if we are judgmental we will likewise be judged;
if we mock God we will reap what we sow;
if we are to be his disciples we must carry the cross and follow him,
and have our old selves crucified with him.
**For Jesus we struggle with these things.**

Holy God, Compassionate and Merciful,
today is a day of remembrance.
A memorial day on which we recall how you proved your love for us,
for while we were still sinners Christ died for us,
fulfilling the prophecy of being wounded for our transgressions,
of being crushed for our iniquities,
of the punishment placed upon him making us whole.
So, we confess our sins, knowing that the One who is faithful and just
will forgive us and cleanse us from all unrighteousness,
for by grace we have been saved through faith,
and this is not of our own doing, but is God's gift to us.
**For us God has done all these things. Amen.**

## This Story (Illumination)

We read again this terrible story
of betrayal, injustice, condemnation and cruelty.
**We read again this astonishing story**
**of divine loving through human suffering.**

We read again this mysterious story,
seeking understanding of the depths of its meaning.
**On this Good Friday, bless our reading and reflecting**
**on this soul-searching, heart-breaking story**
**of the Passion of Christ. Amen.**

**Fear** (Meditation)

*2 Timothy 1:7*

Fear caused all the disciples to flee
when the soldiers came to arrest Jesus.
Fear caused Peter to deny his Lord three times
when he was questioned about being a disciple.
Fear caused the chief priests and leading Pharisees
to falsely accuse Jesus of blasphemy and sedition.
Fear caused Pontius Pilate the Roman Governor
to condemn a man he knew to be innocent.
Their fear brought Jesus to the cross.

But the Spirit of God is a resolute Spirit
and so in the Garden of Gethsemane
Jesus confronted and overcame fear.
"Not my will be done but yours," he prayed.
The Spirit of God is a courageous Spirit,
a Spirit of power and of love and self-discipline.
The Spirit of God helps us follow the example of Jesus
to live sacrificially, faithfully and fearlessly.
His courage brought Jesus to the cross. Amen.

# *Easter Sunday*

### He's the Beginning of Your New Creation (Opening/Gathering)

He's the beginning of your new creation, God,
the first fruits of the harvest you will reap.
**Through his death we are granted redemption,**
**by his life our hope of resurrection is confirmed.**

You burst him out of the tomb where he was buried,
you made him more alive that he had been before.
**Physical life would no longer constrain him,**
**in Spirit form he could now be everywhere.**

Walls and locked doors could not prevent him entering
the upper room where the disciples lodged in fear.
**Sorrowful ones discovered he travelled with them,**
**his presence discovered through the breaking of bread.**

He's the gardener in the new Eden you are planting;
he's the shepherd who leads your flock to pastures green;
**he's the cloud of fire that guides us through the wilderness;**
**he's the signpost showing us the way to you.**

He's the temple calling us here to worship;
he's the messenger whose word is always true.
**He's the righteous ruler who judges justly;**
**he is Jesus, he's our Sovereign and Saviour God. Amen.**

### God Raising God (Praise/Thanksgiving)

*1 Corinthians 5:7-8, 15:20-28; Revelation 5:9-14; Isaiah 53:12;*
*Philippians 2:6-8; Colossians 1:15-21; Hebrews 4:14-16, 12:2;*
*Romans 5:10, 6:4-5*

God raising God, we praise you for the resurrection of Jesus
and the hope of human rebirth that came when he was raised.
We praise you for defeating through Jesus the tyranny of our mortality,
**so while as children of the earth we are subject to death and decay**
**through Christ we are promised new life as the children of God.**

God raising God, we praise you for the resurrection of Jesus
who exercises your sovereign authority in heaven and on earth.
He is the Living Lamb who ransoms saints from every nation,
who is forming a holy priesthood of believers to revere you eternally.
**He is worthy of the worship of all living things in heaven and on earth.**

God raising God, we praise you for the resurrection of Jesus,
your righteous servant, who in turn makes others righteous,
having borne the sins of many and interceded for the transgressors.
**Jesus is your Passover Lamb and the first sheaf of your harvest,
the offering foretold in the rituals of Israel's spring time festivals.**

God raising God, we praise you for the resurrection of Jesus,
the second person of the Trinity, the Creator born the created,
who gave up his power and glory to become a fragile human.
**When through resurrection he became all powerful once again
he became our divine advocate in the hallowed halls of heaven.**

God raising God, we praise you for the resurrection of Jesus,
through whom you reconciled to yourself all things in all creation,
so we may come before you holy, blameless and without reproach.
**Since Jesus understands us, we boldly come to the throne of grace,
there expecting to receive your mercy and help in time of need.**

God raising God, we praise you for the resurrection of Jesus,
the pioneer and perfecter of our faith, who sits at your right hand.
While we were estranged Jesus came to bring us back to you,
and because he lives we have hope of also living life anew.
**We praise you God, and celebrate the resurrection of Jesus. Amen.**

### Familiar Stories (Illumination)

*Luke 24:22-24; Leviticus 23:9-11; 1 Corinthians 15:22-23*

That Jesus who was dead is now alive and lives eternally
is the truth held precious by every Christian believer.
Today we read familiar stories of that first Easter morning;
of women visiting the tomb with spices to anoint the dead,
finding the entrance stone rolled back and the tomb empty,
and having a vision of angels who told them Jesus is alive.
On the day Israel brought its first fruits offering to the temple,
God you raised to life everlasting the first fruits from the dead,
so that all who belong to Christ will in him be made alive.
Today as we read familiar stories of that first Easter morning,
God renew our awe of your astounding love, your amazing grace,
your mighty power, and magnificent plan for humankind,
revealed when you raised Jesus that first Easter morning. Amen.

## Your Greatest Gift to Us (Offering Dedication)

*Romans 5:10*

If we were to impoverish ourselves
by giving everything we own to you God,
we will yet give you only a portion
of all that you have given to us.
Your greatest gift to us is the life,
death and resurrection of Jesus Christ our Lord.
Through his death we are reconciled to you;
through his resurrected life we have salvation.
So in humility we bring our gifts to you,
acknowledging our indebtedness,
and hoping our gifts will support
the work you are doing in the world today.
Bless our gifts by blessing others through them. Amen.

## Easter Blessing (Blessing)

Today, while you celebrate Easter,
as you contemplate the mystery
and meaning of resurrection,
today as you enjoy Easter treats
like hot-cross buns, marsh-mellow eggs,
and hollow chocolate bunnies,
*remember* that Easter reveals God's aroha
through abounding grace restoring life.
May the Gracious God, the Saviour God,
the God who loves you beyond measure,
bless you and yours this holy day
and guide you ever after. Amen.

## Resurrection (Meditation)

An event that has never been duplicated
An event that cannot be logically explained.
An event spoken about only in metaphors.
An event that fundamentally changed the world.

Women come bearing fragrant oils for anointing.
Women find the entrance stone rolled away.
Women find only grave clothes inside the tomb.
Women assume his body has been taken away.

Young men in dazzling white say he has risen.
Young men in dazzling white say he who was dead is now alive.
Young men in dazzling white say tell his disciples the good news.
Young men in dazzling white say he goes before them to Galilee.

A stranger joins mourners on the road to Emmaus.
A stranger explains obscure scriptures to them.
A stranger is invited to share their evening meal.
A stranger's identity becomes known in the breaking of bread.

Disciples fearful bolt the door to their dwelling place.
Disciples startled perceive the risen Christ among them.
Disciples reassured when he says, "Peace be with you."
Disciples fearless when he breaths the Spirit into them.

These are the stories we try to make sense of.
These are the stories we cannot truly understand.
These are the stories we base our faith upon.
These are the stories we deem profoundly true.

Resurrection overcomes death with indestructible life.
Resurrection replaces despair with indescribable joy.
Resurrection annihilates darkness with irresistible light.
Resurrection makes possible a new heaven and earth.

### It's Easter Morning Again (Meditation)

It's Easter morning again
when the new arises out of what was old.
When problems being wrestled with
are suddenly resolved.

It's Easter morning again
when delight expels despair.
When what was lost and broken
is found and is repaired.

It's Easter morning again
when sunshine follows rain.
When the storms of life subside
and peace replaces pain.

It's Easter morning again
when light overwhelms the darkness.
When the bleakness of depression
yields to hope and joyfulness.

Through such moments of renewal
the Easter story gets retold,
of how Jesus emerged to new life
from a sealed tomb dark and cold.

Beautiful is the grace by which
we glimpse God's new creation,
when in our daily lives we see
these signs of resurrection.

## Mary's Witness (Meditation)

*John 20:1-18; Matthew 27:55-61, 28:1-2*

The sun sank down below the horizon
darkness descended and the first stars appeared.
Her Sabbath of mourning had finally ended,
time now to do women's work,
to prepare the spices for anointing the dead.

Mary Magdalene and some other women
had stayed by Jesus throughout his ordeal,
far enough away to be ignored by the soldiers,
close enough for him to know they were there.
This vigil they kept until he was removed from the cross.

Sitting across from the tomb they watched his interment,
but couldn't see Joseph and Nicodemus hastily discharge
the burial customs for a Jew of high standing.
So early in the morning on the first day of the week
they came carrying spices for anointing the dead.

The earth shook, the entrance stone rolled back.
Where his body had been was only his shroud
and nearby the cloth that had covered his head.
Run tell Peter, "They have taken our Lord out of the tomb,
and we don't know where they have laid him."

"Woman why are you weeping? Whom are you seeking?"
Only when he said "Mary" did she perceive who was speaking.
The tomb was empty because Jesus has risen.
Run tell the disciples, "I have seen the Lord!
He's ascending to his Father and our Father, his God and our God."

# *Good Shepherd Sunday*

## Great Redeemer Shepherd (Opening/Gathering)

*Ezekiel 34:25-31; John 10:1-5; Psalm 23:1-3; Isaiah 40:10-11*

God you are our shepherd and we the sheep of your pasture.
**We know your voice, we have heard you calling us to gather.**

You lead to us to lands of lush pasture and beside streams of pure water.
**You nourish us with your Word and with your Spirit
you refresh our souls.**

You have made a covenant of peace with us and given us security.
**Today, as we worship you, may what we say and sing
be acceptable in your hearing, Great Redeemer Shepherd. Amen.**

## We Need Servant Leaders (Intercession)

*Ezekiel 34:1-10, 31; Isaiah 55:11; John 10:12, 16; Proverbs 11:14; 12:19;
Matthew 20:25-27; Luke 22:24-27; Psalm 95:7; 100:3*

God you chose Israel in ancient times to be your special sheep,
but you made clear through Jesus that you have other flocks.
Every person, every tribe, every nation is equally precious to you.
You want everyone to live well the life that you have given them.

God too many people have hirelings not shepherds leading them.
People who feed on the sheep rather than provide for them.
Autocratic leaders and their enablers who make themselves rich
through corruption and the exploitation of the people they lead.

Jesus warned about leaders who dictatorially lord it over people
and call themselves benefactors while benefitting only themselves.
We have too many leaders who fit this description in the world today
and we have too many people cruelly suffering because of them.

God we need servant leaders of the type Jesus spoke about,
who put the welfare of the people far above their own interests,
who wisely seek wise counsel before making major decisions,
and who always speak the truth even when the truth hurts them.

God you are God of all, and we are all the sheep of your pasture.
You see the harm being done to those being led astray by lies.
We look to you to raise up courageous truth telling prophets
like those who condemned the behaviour of Israel's ruling classes.

God help us change the world by changing those in charge,
by replacing greedy hirelings with shepherds who serve the sheep.
May all the people in the world have opportunities to prosper,
by being led by shepherds who work at doing good for them. Amen.

### Our Good Shepherd (Illumination)

Loving God, the scriptures speak of you as our Good Shepherd,
a metaphor that has lost its potency for us modern people.
Those of us who live in cities have little contact with farm animals,
and on our farms shepherds no longer live with their sheep.
As we examine the ancient texts, help us enter the Biblical world,
that we may perceive the ageless message these scriptures contain,
especially the texts that depict you as our Good Shepherd. Amen.

### Beyond the Sheepfold's Gates (Offering Dedication)

*Isaiah 40:11; John 10:16*

Great God who feeds your flock like a shepherd,
who gathers your lambs up into your arms,
holding them close against your chest,
and who gently leads the adult sheep at your feet,
we give you thanks for your bountiful provision,
and bring our gifts to support your other sheep.
Bless these offerings for the work of your flock
within these walls and beyond the sheepfold's gates. Amen.

### Your Faithful Shepherd (Blessing)

*Isaiah 40:11, 53:6; Ezekiel 34:15-16; Psalm 23:1-6; Luke 15:1-7;
John 7:37-38, 14:1-3*

While like sheep we tend to go astray,
we have a Faithful Shepherd who will
seek for and find us when we're lost.
So should you choose a pathway in life
that takes you in the wrong direction,
know your Shepherd will go after you
and will carry you back home rejoicing.
May you follow his lead to green pastures,
may your soul be restored by living waters,
may his grace and his mercy always pursue you,
and bring you to his holy dwelling place. Amen.

# *Ascension*

## Citizens of Heaven, Ambassadors for Christ (Opening/Gathering)

*Ephesians 2:19-22; 1 Peter 2:5; Revelation 3:5; Matthew 6:10;
Hebrews 4:14-16, 8:1-2, 12:22-24; Luke 24:50-53; 1 Peter 2:9;
John 15:26, 16:7; 2 Corinthians 5:20*

We are citizens in the household of the Holy One,
we are living stones in the dwelling place of God.
**We are a chosen people, a royal priesthood gathered
in worship of God our Father, who is judge of all.**

Singing songs of praise we enter the holy temple of heaven,
in prayer we boldly come into the throne room of God,
**where the Son sits at the right hand of the Father
and is the high priest who mediates on our behalf.**

For this he was incarnated, for this he was crucified,
and ascended into heaven after he was resurrected.
**Now our names are recorded in God's Book of Life,
of those who seek to do God's will here on earth.**

On this Ascension Day, we praise the Son our Saviour,
who because of his departure could send to be with us,
**the Holy Spirit, the Truth Teller and Comforter,
to whom we give thanks for being our Holy Advocate.**

We are citizens of heaven, ambassadors for Christ,
and in worship we have come to the heavenly Jerusalem,
**where with angels and the spirits of the righteous made perfect
we join our voices in praise of the Holy Living God. Amen.**

## The Ascended Christ (Opening/Gathering)

*1 Peter 2:9; Luke 24:50-51; John 17:1-5; Ephesians 1:20; Acts 1:10-11*

Today we gather as the people of God,
called out of darkness by Jesus the Christ.
**Today we worship the ascended Christ.**

Today we come seeking to better know God
and Jesus the Christ whom God sent to earth.
**Today we worship the glorified Christ.**

Today we come into the presence of God
and the One who sits at God's right hand.
**Today we worship the majestic Christ.**

Today we seek to learn from the One
who came from God and went back to God,
who someday will return in the same way he left.
**Today we worship our Lord and Saviour,**
**Jesus the risen, eternal Christ. Amen.**

## By the Holy Spirit (Confession)

*Acts 1:6-11; Matthew 28:19-20; 10:20; John 13:34-35, 14:2-3, 18, 26;*
*1 John 4:7-13; Romans 8:11, 14, 12:6-8; 1 Peter 2:9*

The disciples were told to wait.
To wait for the promise of the Father,
to wait to be baptised by the Holy Spirit.

Sometimes God we need to be like the disciples.
To wait on the promises you have made to us,
to wait for the stirrings of the Holy Spirit.

Sometimes God we need to stop waiting.
To redirect our gaze from the sky to the earth,
to respond to the promptings of the Holy Spirit.

The disciples were told to be your witnesses,
from Judaea to the ends of the earth
as they were empowered by the Holy Spirit.

We too are called to be your witnesses,
to follow and proclaim the teachings of Christ
as brought to mind by the Holy Spirit.

Sometimes we live up to our calling.
We faithfully follow Jesus' commandment to love,
and we channel to others the love of the Holy Spirit.

Sometimes we ignore the great commission.
We fail to live as disciple making disciples,
we fail to use the gifts given us by the Holy Spirit.

Jesus said his disciples would not be orphaned.
He would not depart and leave them bereaved.
After he left he would send them the Holy Spirit.

We too are not orphans but the children of God,
chosen to proclaim the mighty acts of God,
given new life through the indwelling Holy Spirit.

God, forgive us for our many inadequacies,
for the times we fail to live up to our holy vocation.
Light us up with the fire of the Holy Spirit.

On this day when we ponder the ascension of Christ,
and are anticipating the events of Pentecost,
full us once more with the joy of the Holy Spirit.

On this day when we ponder Jesus coming again
we give thanks that he is preparing a place for us,
and that he is where we are through the Holy Spirit. Amen.

### The Law, the Prophets, and the Psalms (Illumination)

*Luke 24:44-53*

During the period between his resurrection and his ascension
the Risen Christ periodically appeared to his disciples,
reminding them of what he had previously told them,
that in the Law of Moses, the prophets, and the psalms
they would find scriptures that pointed to him,
foretelling of his suffering and his resurrection.
Just as he opened their minds to comprehend the sacred texts,
may we also grow in our understanding of the scriptures,
when we read and reflect upon the story of his departing,
during our commemoration of the ascension of the Risen Christ. Amen.

### We Bring Gifts (Offering Dedication)

*Matthew 28:18-20; Mark 16:19-20; Acts 1:8-9*

Jesus you were vindicated by your resurrection,
by being restored to the former glory you had.
You ascended back to the throne of God
and were given authority over heaven and earth.
You commissioned the first members of your church
to teach the world what you had taught them.
You told them to take the gospel to every nation,
starting in Jerusalem and going to the ends of the earth.
We are their successors and have the same obligation.
So we bring gifts we ask you to bless for the work
of your church in this place in our far distant land. Amen.

## The One Who Sits at God's Right Hand (Blessing)

*Mark 16:19; Matthew 28:20; Romans 8:34; 1 John 3:23*

May the one who sits at God's right hand
also sit beside you in loving companionship.
When you are in need of encouragement
may you perceive his gentle reassurance.
When you are in need of a fresh direction
may you receive his compassionate guidance.
When you are in need of hope and confidence
may you truly believe what he says to you,
"I am with you always, to the end of the age."
So may the risen and ascended one,
who came from God and has gone back to God,
to be your intercessor at the throne of heaven,
bless you today and every day as you believe in his name
and love his people as he commanded. Amen.

## Forty is Not Human Time (Meditation)

*Genesis 7:12, 8:5-7; Exodus 24:18; Numbers 13:25, 14:34; Joshua 5:10-12; Judges 5:31, 8:28; 1 Samuel 4:17-18, 17:16; 1 Kings 19:8; Matthew 4:1-2; Acts 1:3*

Forty days of rain to flood Noah's world,
then many more days waiting for the water to subside;
and when the top of the mountainous ziggurats appeared,
Noah released a raven after waiting forty days.

Forty days of wondering Moses' fate on the mountain side,
time enough to write a law and craft a golden calf.
Forty days of spying out the land of the Canaanites,
long enough to terrify both spies and Israelites.

Forty years of following a cloud of smoke and fire,
forty years of hardship, on their way to the Promised Land,
and having lived on manna every day for forty years
they finally crossed the Jordan and ate the produce of the land.

Joshua succeeded Moses, and the judges after him.
Their people experienced conflict as they colonised the land.
Gideon and Deborah led Israel out against the foe,
and following their victories the land rested forty years.

When the Ark was captured Eli died having judged for forty years,
then Samuel administered justice until Israel desired a king.
In the days of Saul, Goliath mocked Israel for forty days
until felled by a stone slung by an indignant shepherd boy.

The first three kings of Israel each reigned for forty years,
but after them no one man ruled over all twelve tribes again.
Elijah fled from Jezebel who vowed to have him killed.
He encountered God at Sinai after walking forty days.

Before Jesus began his ministry in Herod's Galilee,
the devil tried to tempt him after he'd fasted forty days.
For forty days from Easter day the risen Christ appeared
until within the cloud of glory he ascended from human view.

Forty is not human time, measurable in minutes and in hours.
Forty is God's blessing time, beyond human quantifying.
Forty is transition time, between what was and what is to be.
Forty is kingdom time, when God's purposes are revealed.

# *Week of Prayer for Christian Unity*

**United in Diversity** (Opening/Gathering)

With all the saints gathered here among us,
**and with all the saints assembled elsewhere;**

with all the other saints in our community,
**and with all the saints who live far away;**

with all the saints of our tradition,
**and with all the saints of other denominations;**

we come before you to offer our worship,
**we come before you seeking your grace.**

Bless the worship of your people today.
**Bless your church united in its diversity. Amen.**

## The Barriers that Divide (Confession)

*John 8:31-32, 13:34-35, 17:20-21*

Jesus you prayed that we would be one;
one with you and one with your Father,
and clearly in harmony with one another.
Jesus too often we have divided and divided,
when we've argued about theology and liturgy,
over what each of us think we know about you
and about what we think you want us to do.
**God – Father, Son and Holy Spirit – forgive us.**

Jesus you commanded us to love like you;
to show the world that we are your disciples
by our outgoing regard and mutual respect
overcoming discord over different perspectives.
Jesus we have too often become bitter,
insisting on our status as true believers
while disparaging others for their beliefs.
**God – Father Son and Holy Spirit – forgive us.**

Jesus, you told us that to truly be disciples
we must live according to your teachings,
then we would know the truth that frees
us from our prejudices and self-righteousness.
Jesus we have too often chosen persuasive leaders
who offer us well-being if we just follow them,
and we have failed to take up our cross to follow you.
**God – Father, Son and Holy Spirit – forgive us.**

Jesus, bless our efforts to be ecumenical;
to break down the barriers that once divided us,
to understand that we are all imperfect servants,
with incomplete knowledge of you and your ways.
Help us welcome your reign as we worship together
and to work as one to care for the earth and the poor.
May together we demonstrate the power of your grace.
**God – Father, Son and Holy Spirit – bless us. Amen.**

## God You Call Us (Intercession)

*1 John 2:9-10, 4:20-21; Matthew 7:3-5, 28:19-20; Hebrews 12:14;*
*1 Peter 2:9; 2 Peter 1:18*

God you call us into a relationship with you
through our relationships with one another.
We cannot claim to love you God when
we harbour bitterness against a sister.
We cannot say we walk in your light when
we stumble in the darkness of despising a brother.
Help us to be too busy correcting our own faults
to have time to criticise the failings of others.

God you call us to demonstrate your love
through the love we have for one another.
We cannot claim you to be the God of peace
when we are in strife with other believers.
We cannot say you are the God of harmony
when we only respect disciples who are like us.
Help us to see our differing perspectives as
opportunities to grow in grace and knowledge.

God you call us to be your special people,
to proclaim to the world your mighty acts.
We cannot claim to be your holy nation
when the world too clearly sees our discord.
We cannot say we are a royal priesthood
when we don't live up to the gospel's values.
Help us to see your mission requires us to
worship and work cooperatively together. Amen.

# *Day of Pentecost*

**Love Came Down** (Opening/Gathering)

*Romans 8:8-9; Deuteronomy 16:9-12, 26:10-12; Acts 2:1-13, 37-47*

Love came down on Sinai amidst the smoke and fire.
A covenant of love was made and a law of love was given.
**The one who loves another has fulfilled the law's demands.**

Love came down at harvest time when the grain was gathered in.
God was praised for God's provision at a festival of thanksgiving.
**Love insisted the Lord's bounty be shared with those in need.**

Love came down on Pentecost upon the first Jesus believers.
Pilgrims heard the gospel, proclaimed in their mother tongues.
**Believers shared all they had, and God added to their number.**

Love comes down every Pentecost to every Jesus follower.
Love goes out into the world through the Church's open doors.
**Loving Spirit, Holy Spirit, you are always welcome here. Amen.**

**When the Holy Spirit Came** (Offering Dedication)

*Acts 2:45-47*

On Pentecost when the Holy Spirit came
the apostles were emboldened to speak
of all that Jesus had done for humanity.
Today your church continues to proclaim
the same good news of his saving grace.
Remembering how the first believers
shared their wealth with those in need,
this Pentecost we bring our offerings
in support of the work of the church,
and to help people in our community
with insufficient income to live on.
God bless these gifts given with glad
and generous hearts full of praise of you,
and bless your church with the goodwill
of the people among whom we dwell,
as you did when the church was young,
after the Holy Spirit came at Pentecost. Amen.

## On Pentecost (Offering Dedication)

*Leviticus 23:15-17; Acts 2:1-36*

Generous God, on Pentecost the people baked loaves to give to you
made of wheat from the harvest that you had lately given them.
Guiding God, on Pentecost the Jesus believers assembled in one place
remembering the instructions the Risen Christ had given them.
Glorious God, on Pentecost the disciples began preaching the gospel
being emboldened by the Spirit you had just given them.
Gracious God, this Pentecost we bring our freewill offerings to you
acknowledging joyfully with gratitude all you have given us.
Bless these gifts donated for the functioning of your church
and to provide sustenance for those in need of bread. Amen.

## May the Spirit... (Blessing)

May the Spirit who hovered over the primordial water
bringing into being abundant life on earth
bring light and fruitfulness to our lives.
May the Spirit that appeared as a column of cloud and fire
leading the Israelites through the wilderness
lead us in our daily walk of faith.
May the Spirit that filled the first temple with glory
and came with signs of power to the first church in Jerusalem
fill us with God life, that we may be truly blessed.
And so may God – Father, Son and Spirit –
be with us now and forever. Amen.

## Empowered by the Spirit (Commissioning)

*Acts 2:1-4, 17-18; Romans 8:6; 2 Timothy 1:7; John 16:13*

May the Spirit who came upon the disciples on Pentecost
empower you as the Spirit empowered them for God's work.
Set your mind on the Spirit which for you is life and peace,
for the Spirit who was poured out on the day of Pentecost
is not a Spirit of timidity but of strength and courage,
not the Spirit of acrimony but of love and harmony,
not the Spirit of error but of truth and understanding,
who instils in the believer confidence in God's promises.
May the Spirit who appeared as tongues of fire on Pentecost
enable you to live according to the teachings of Jesus
so that you may be a witness to God's presence in the world. Amen

## Partner With the Spirit (Meditation)

*Acts 2:17-18*

Sons and daughters prophesy of a world of peace and love.
Young men imagine a world where everyone can prosper.
Old men dream hopeful dreams for a world that's yet to be.
Young women foresee a bright future for yourself and your family.
Old women visualise a world where everyone is free.
Let's all dream these big dreams of how the world might be
were we to live together with compassion and generosity,
if we were to partner with the Spirit, poured forth at Pentecost,
and truly follow the teachings of the one who is the Christ.

## The Day You Began Your Church (Meditation)

*Acts 2:1-42; Leviticus 23:15-21; Exodus 19:16-19, 20:1-21; Psalm 119;*
*Ruth 4:13, 17; Joel 2:28-30*

God on the day when your people were offering
leavened loaves and lambs in thanksgiving
for the harvest they were bringing in,
the grain from which to bake their daily bread,
**on that day you began your church.**

God on the day when your people were recalling
the fire and the thunder of your descent
on Mount Sinai when you gave them the law,
commandments by which to live in community,
**on that day you began your church.**

God on the day when your people were reciting
the psalms of David, the sweet singer of Israel,
who according to folklore was born on Pentecost,
and remembering Ruth, his Moabite ancestor,
**on that day you began your church.**

God on the day when your people were longing
for the fulfilment of ancient prophecies
promising an outpouring of your Holy Spirit,
transforming both old and young into visionaries,
**on that day you began your church.**

God on the day when your people were gathered
from throughout the world to worship you,
when one hundred and twenty followers of Jesus
were assembled together with one accord,
**on that day you began your church.**

God on the day when you blew into Jerusalem
manifesting your presence in tongues of fire,
pilgrims heard the gospel in their own languages,
and three thousand believed and were baptised,
**on that day you began your church.**

God on the day when your people kept Pentecost
and down through the centuries ever since,
your Spirit has been inspiring faithful believers to
boldly proclaim your gospel of hope, as was done
**on that day you began your church. Amen.**

### Pentecost in Winter (Meditation)

In our land Pentecost comes in winter
when we venture outdoors wrapped in coats and beanies,
scarves and mittens
and hear the crunch of frost stiffened grass underfoot,
and know that the sun will shine brightly on this winter's day.

In our land Pentecost comes in winter
when wrapped in the warmth of the Spirit's love,
we venture forth into life knowing that
**the Son of Righteousness shines brightly upon us this Pentecost day.**

In our land Pentecost comes in winter
when we wear gumboots to protect our feet from muddy soil
and hold overhead umbrellas to keep us dry from the rain
that seeps deep into the ground to hydrate seeds sprouting into life.

In our land Pentecost comes in winter
when sheltered under the Spirit's canopy
we go forth into life knowing that living water fills
**the well of salvation, from which we draw this Pentecost day.**

In our land Pentecost comes in winter
when snow falls silently and transforms the landscape
with magical whiteness,
when farmers feed out hay to nourish sheep and cows and deer,
and when with excitement city folk drive to the mountains
with skis on car roof racks.

In our land Pentecost comes in winter
when like freshly fallen snow the Spirit's mercy covers our sinfulness,
and nurtured by the promises of God
**we rejoice in being forgiven people this Pentecost day.**

In our land Pentecost comes in winter
when storms blow off roofs and upend trees and rivers swell
into raging torrents.
In awe of the power of the wind and the rain
we go out to repair the damage,
and sand bag against engulfing flood waters.

In our land Pentecost comes in winter
when the Spirit sweeps powerfully through our lives
uprooting and drowning all not of God and
**we know our hearts to have been be renewed this Pentecost day. Amen.**

# *Trinity Sunday*

## One God, God Three in One (Opening/Gathering)

One God, God Three in One,
God of mighty mystery,
God the Holy Trinity,
**we gather here to worship you**

Loving God, God of empathy,
God that draws us into you,
Parent, Brother, Spirit Friend,
**we gather here to honour you.**

God we hardly comprehend,
God of divine complexity,
One God, God Three in One,
**we gather here in praise of you,**
**God the Holy Trinity. Amen.**

## Expressions of Our Love (Opening/Gathering)

Holy Trinity, you who dwell in a circle of mutual love
drawing us to you and surrounding us with your love,
**may you find in our praying and in our singing this morning**
**expressions of our love for you.**

Holy Trinity, you who dwell in a circle of mutual love
drawing us into loving relationships with others,
**may you find in our acts of generosity and kindness this day**
**expressions of our love for you.**

Holy Trinity, you who dwell in a circle of mutual love
drawing us into living harmoniously with earth's ecosystems,
**may you find in our growing concern for all living things**
**expressions of our love for you.**

Holy Trinity, you who dwell in a circle of mutual love
drawing us into the wisdom that infuses your teaching,
**may you find in our dedication to discipleship**
**expressions of our love for you. Amen.**

## The Harm We Personally Have Done (Confession)

*James 3:13-18; Matthew 5:24; John 13:34; Luke 22:25-27;*
*1 Thessalonians 5:19; Romans 8:14, 26-27*

Parenting God, forgive us for being unruly children.
We have not treasured the treasures you have given us.
Rather we have caused the extinction of living things.
We have not lived in harmony with one another.
Rather we have lived the way of strife and exploitation.
**Triune God forgive us the harm we personally have done.**

Teaching God, forgive us for being inattentive students.
We have ignored the instructions you have given us.
We often put seeking after wealth ahead of seeking after you.
We fail to keep your commandment to love one another.
We often don't serve others but we expect them to serve us.
**Triune God forgive us the harm we personally have done.**

Shepherding God, forgive us for being unfaithful followers.
We often don't respond to your promptings to do the right thing.
Rather we go our own way regardless of the consequences.
We often don't seek your help in overcoming our weaknesses.
Rather we rely on our own flawed thinking and inadequate willpower.
**Triune God forgive us the harm we personally have done.**

God, Parent, Teacher, Advocate, we give you grateful thanks
that in spite of our many failings your love for us never falters.
We know you will always respond in mercy when we pray,
**Triune God forgive us the harm we personally have done. Amen.**

## We Cannot Know the Mystery of Your Being (Illumination)

God we cannot know the mystery of your being.
We cannot understand how you are Three in One.
We can only vaguely speak of you in metaphors,
while aware our perception of you is much too small.
God we know of you through creation and the scriptures,
the holy words which your people wrote so long ago,
to express what the Spirit stirred within them
to believe about their God, the Trinity.
Open up our hearts today to your instruction.
Help us marvel once more at the wonder of your grace.
Bless our reading and reflecting on your scriptures.
Help us comprehend what we haven't understood before. Amen.

## You who Inspired Prophets (Illumination)

Father, Son, Holy Spirit, you
who inspired prophets, apostles, songwriters and sages
to write of their encounters with you,
help us to hear what you have to say to us today
in the words they wrote long ago.
Help us to reflect on those words wisely
and grow in our understanding of you Triune God. Amen.

## God our Creator, Our Saviour, Our Advocate (Offering Dedication)

*John 17:20-23*

God our Creator, Our Saviour, Our Advocate
We bring offerings in worship of you
to express our gratitude for
an earth rich in resources;
to express our thankfulness for
a gospel rich in hopefulness;
to express appreciation for
your restoration of our brokenness
fulfilling your promise to us of abundant life.

We bring offerings in worship of you
to express our gratitude for
being made in your image,
so that we may be in relationship with you;
to express our thankfulness for
being recipients of your wisdom,
so that we may live freely and fearlessly;
to express our appreciation for
the bonding presence of the Holy Spirit,
so that by our unity with you and with one another
the world will come to know who Jesus truly is. Amen.

**Go Back Into the World** (Commissioning)

Go back into the world, knowing that
God is an affectionate Parent,
God is an understanding Messiah,
God is a compassionate Comforter.

Go back into the world, knowing that
God the Holy Trinity is calling and equipping you
to live lovingly, to behave graciously
and to speak wisely, this day and every day.

Go back into the world, knowing that
in your going you take with you the blessing of
the eternal, the merciful, the tender-hearted God,
who is the Father, the Son, and the Holy Spirit. Amen.

# Ordinary Time

### Loving God Hear Us (Opening/Gathering)

Loving God hear us,
when in praise we speak of you,
in our words take pleasure,
**for you alone we worship God**
**unto you our prayers ascend.**

Redeemer God hear us,
when we come in prayer to you,
of our words take notice,
**for you alone can save us God,**
**upon you we must depend.**

Compassionate God encourage us,
when our hearts cry out to you,
in our words hear our distress,
**for you alone supply the faith**
**to overcome our fears.**

Merciful God be with us,
when we seek to understand
show your holy ways to us,
**for you alone can school us God**
**on the wonders of your grace.**

Gracious God be with us,
when we come together
bless all those gathered here,
**for you alone can form us God**
**into the church of our living Lord. Amen.**

## Jesus You Tell Us (Opening/Gathering)

*Mark 1:15*

Jesus you tell us that the time is fulfilled.
**The kingdom of God has come near to us.**

Jesus you tell us it's time to believe.
**We rejoice in the gospel God brings to us.**

Jesus you call upon us to repent.
**God lovingly reconciles us and gives us hope.**

Jesus you teach us to follow your way.
**Bless your disciples gathered to worship today. Amen.**

## Week by Week we Gather (Opening/Gathering)

Week by week we gather to
pray, to sing, to hear the gospel story.
**This is what we call worship.**

Week by week we gather
in acknowledgement of our mutual belief
in the divine Someone who is greater than us,
who co-authors with us the stories of our lives.
**This is what we call worship.**

Week by week we gather.
Week by week we worship.
**Bless our gathering and our worship today. Amen.**

## The Blessing of Assembling To Worship (Opening/Gathering)

We come together each week
in a regular rhythm of worship.
**In the company of friends we gather
to meet with God our Parent again.**

We sing words of praise and thanksgiving
for all God the Son has done.
**We offer up words of petition
for what we hope God the Spirit will do.**

We read and reflect on the scriptures
listening for what God has to say.
**We come knowing the blessing
of assembling together to worship today. Amen.**

## Today We Light the Christ Candle (Candle lighting)

Today we light the Christ Candle
in honour of the One who brings light to the world.
**Lord bring light to all who are in places of darkness.**

Today we light the Christ Candle
in honour of the One who brings the gift of abundant life.
**Lord protect all whose lives are threatened by violence and famine.**

Today we light the Christ Candle
in honour of the One who redeems the world.
**Lord deliver the world from evil, and us from complacency.**

Today we light the Christ Candle
in honour of the One who revealed the Father
and sent the Spirit to be our Advocate.
**May our worship today be pleasing to the Triune God. Amen.**

## Lighting the Candle for Healing (Candle lighting)

Sorrow and sickness afflicts our world.
**We light the candle praying for healing.**

Despair and destruction afflicts our world.
**We light the candle praying for healing.**

Injury and injustice afflicts our world.
**We light the candle praying for healing.**

Crisis and conflict afflicts our world.
**We light the candle praying for healing.**

We are heart-broken over the suffering in the world.
**We light the candle praying for healing. Amen.**

**We Praise and Glorify Your Name** (Praise/Thanksgiving)

Everlasting God,
you are the one who
will be what you will be,
and do what you will do,
unbounded in power and purpose.
**We praise and glorify your name.**

Unfathomable God,
you are the one who is
immense beyond our imagination
majestic beyond our comprehension
astonishing beyond our appreciation.
**We praise and glorify your name.**

Holy God,
you are the one who is
worshipped by the hosts of heaven,
revered above all sacred things,
enthroned on the praises of your people.
**We praise and glorify your name.**

Righteous God
you are the one who
judges justly and acts fairly,
does not forget the cry of the afflicted,
and is a stronghold for the oppressed.
**We praise and glorify your name.**

Faithful God,
you are the one who
keeps all your promises,
and upholds all your covenants,
who speaks words of truth and fulfils them.
**We praise and glorify your name.**

Merciful God
You are the one who
remembers our frailty,
pardons our impiety,
kerbs our stupidity.
**We praise and glorify your name.**

Loving God
you are the one who
came to earth to teach us,
came to earth to save us.
Came to earth to show us
**how to praise and glorify your name. Amen.**

## Loving God, Our Divine Parent (Praise/Thanksgiving)

Loving God, our divine parent,
tenderly caring for all your children,
making no distinction between race or creed, status or ability.
*We thank you for loving us so kind-heartedly.*

Loving God, our devoted spouse,
jealously treasuring your beloved bride the church,
overlooking her imperfections, mercifully forgiving her sins.
*We thank you for loving us so completely.*

Loving God, our servant sovereign,
ruling over us with great gentleness
remembering our frailness and vulnerability.
*We thank you for loving us so compassionately.*

Loving God, our Parent, Bridegroom, Monarch,
in worship we respond with awe to the wonder
of your love, your devotion, your generosity.
*We thank you for loving us so graciously. Amen.*

## The Truth that Sets Us Free (Confession)

*John 8:31-36*

It's not just any truth that sets us free
but the truth contained within your word,
which if we faithfully follow will free
us from the bondage of erroneous beliefs.

The error of thinking we can be totally self-reliant
and have no need for the blessings of God.
It is not just our bodies that need refreshing,
our souls need to be fed by the word of God.

The error of thinking our ways are always right
and we have no need for divine instruction.
Our damaged world shows our lack of judgment,
that the choices we make are often not good.

The error of thinking we are in complete control,
that the earth is ours to dominate and exploit.
Disease epidemics and other natural disasters
prove beyond doubt how vulnerable we are.

God help us embrace the truth that frees us
from the deceptions of human arrogance.
Everyone who commits sin is a slave to sin,
but when the Son makes us free we are free indeed. Amen.

## We Were Designed to Worship (Confession)

*Romans 1:19-23*

We were designed to worship.
If we don't worship you God we will worship something else.
We'll pursue fame and fortune and then discover that wealth
provides many possessions but does not bring happiness,
and fame means our names and faces are so well known
that we have to imprison ourselves in order to have privacy.

**We were designed to worship.**
If we don't worship you God we will worship something else.
We'll pursue a great love affair or a great career and discover
relationships can become fraught and being fragile don't last,
for our deepest desires cannot be met by another person,
while the careers we pursue just consume the hours of our lives.

**We were designed to worship.**
If we don't worship you God we will worship something else.
We'll elevate the importance of our own intellect and discover
that we are not nearly as clever as we imagine ourselves to be.
We'll try to create for ourselves a world where you don't exist
and instead of exalting humanity we'll make humanity insignificant.

**We were designed to worship.**
God you don't need our worship, but we need to worship you.
For when we worship the creation instead of the Creator
we end up diminishing ourselves and undervaluing creation,
and we are without excuse for since the cosmic big bang
your power and divinity has been evident from what came to exist.

**We were designed to worship.**
God even when we commit ourselves to worshipping you alone,
we are sometimes guilty of worshipping things other than you.
We seek your forgiveness, asking you to restore us and
remind us of your design in designing us to worship you. Amen.

**Freedom** (Confession)

*John 8:31-32*

Lord God, we pray for freedom.
We pray for freedom from the prejudice,
that prevents us from seeing others as they truly are,
that prevents others from seeing us as we truly are.
**We pray for healing from the blindness of prejudice.**

Lord God, we pray for freedom.
We pray for freedom from the scornfulness,
that causes us to speak sneeringly of others,
that causes others to speak sneeringly of us.
**We pray for healing from the wounding of scornfulness.**

Lord God, we pray for freedom.
We pray for freedom from the belligerency,
that draws us into conflict with others,
that draws others into conflict with us.
**We pray for healing from the infection of belligerency.**

Lord God, we pray for freedom.
We pray for freedom from the hypocrisy,
that afflicts our self-righteousness upon others,
that afflicts the self-righteousness of others upon us.
**We pray for healing from the disease of hypocrisy.**

Lord God, we pray for freedom.
We pray for freedom from the dogmatism,
that keeps us from hearing the wisdom of others,
that keeps others from hearing the wisdom we have.
**We pray for healing from the deafness of dogmatism.**

Lord God, we pray for freedom.
The freedom that comes through the teaching of Jesus,
that shows us how to be loving towards others,
that shows others how to be loving towards us.
**We pray for the healing of the gospel of Christ. Amen.**

## We Desire to Speak Words of Wisdom (Confession)

*James 3:3-13*

Lord, our desire is to speak words of wisdom,
but instead too often we say foolish things.
**Forgive our speaking.**

Lord our intention is to speak words of truth,
but instead too often we withhold some of the truth.
**Forgive our silence.**

Lord we plan to think carefully before we speak,
but instead too often what we say is careless and harmful.
**Forgive our speaking.**

Lord we wish to proclaim the gospel,
but instead not knowing what to say we say nothing at all.
**Forgive our silence.**

Lord when we speak in ways that lead to
strife rather than harmony,
resentment rather than reconciliation,
grief rather than consolation,
**forgive our speaking.**

Lord, grant us wisdom to speak wisely,
courage to speak truthfully,
compassion to speak kindly,
**and when words fail us
may our loving actions witness to you.**

For we remember that you are the
Holy One who made us in your image
to be in relationship with you
and to live as holy people.

**You are the Word that came among us
to teach us the truth that sets us free.**
You are the Holy Spirit sent to guide us,
inspiring scriptures to encourage and correct.

Lord, forgive our speaking when it is hurtful
and our silence when it harms the hurting.
**Teach us to speak words of wisdom
and to know when it is wise not to speak.**

Lord we are assured of your forgiveness
and thankful for your instruction.
**We praise you for the wisdom of your words. Amen.**

## Walls and Bridges (Confession)

We have a choice to build walls or bridges;
to shut ourselves away from other people
or to invite them into fellowship with us.
**God inspire us to build bridges not walls.**

We have a choice to build walls or bridges;
to feed our prejudices against other races
or to experience cultures different to ours.
**God inspire us to build bridges not walls.**

We have a choice to build walls or bridges;
to construct barriers to keep out refugees
or to help them find a new home with us.
**God inspire us to build bridges not walls.**

We have a choice to build walls or bridges;
to insist that we alone know the way to God
or to be open to the insights of other faiths.
**God inspire us to build bridges not walls.**

We have a choice to build walls or bridges;
to condemn the poor for their own misfortune
or to work for social change to help them thrive.
**God inspire us to build bridges not walls.**

We have a choice to build walls or bridges;
to judge harshly those who have made mistakes
or to recognise that we also are guilty of sin.
**God inspire us to build bridges not walls.**

We have a choice to build walls or bridges;
to reject people who live on the margins
or welcome them into the centre with us.
**God inspire us to build bridges not walls.**

We have a choice to build walls or bridges;
to exclude the impure like the Pharisees
or to seek out lepers and sinners like Jesus.
**God inspire us to build bridges not walls.**

Too often we chose to build walls not bridges.
Too often we close our hearts to the needy.
Call us to repentance and grant us forgiveness.
**God inspire us to build bridges not walls. Amen.**

## Exploring the Scriptures (Illumination)

Every time we read the scriptures
we travel back to a far distant time,
to a culture that has long disappeared,
to a people with a vastly different world view
to how we perceive the world to be.
Yet we share a common humanity,
and the gospel that resonated with them,
continues to give meaning to our lives.

Every time we read the scriptures
we come seeking divine revelation,
the essence of truth that never changes
no matter how many millennia go by.
God be our guide as we go exploring
the wisdom contained in the scriptures,
and help us mine for the nuggets of insight
that will enrich our lives beyond measure. Amen

## Open the Scriptures to Our Understanding (Illumination)

God open the scriptures to our understanding.
Grant us the wisdom to see within the text
the eternal truths of your love and graciousness.
God open the scriptures to our understanding.
Grant us the wisdom to respond in love and graciousness
to the message you have for us in the
scriptures read and reflected upon today. Amen.

## The Relevance of Your Ancient Word (Illumination)

God help us to see the relevance
of your ancient word to our modern lives.
Help us to perceive the principles
that are as true today as in bygone times.
Help us take to heart your judgments
given to people long ago that also apply to us.
Help us be uplifted by your promises
that encouraged those who have travelled
before us the road that we are now on.
God open our minds to the ageless truths
contained within the scriptures we read today. Amen

## Coming Closer to God through the Scriptures (Illumination)

Gracious God, we come to your scriptures
hoping that through them we will come closer to you.
We see evidence of your love and mercy
in these words written long ago
to a people of a different culture to ours
who lived in environments not like ours,
but whose experience resonates with us,
for what you were yesterday,
you are today and will be tomorrow, forever our
Gracious Saviour, our Loving Lord, our Faithful Friend.
Grant us deeper insight into the words read and reflected upon today,
and through these words bring us closer to you. Amen.

## Speak to Us (Illumination)

Speak to us through your words God.
Speak plainly so that we can comprehend.
Speak compellingly so that we will hearken.
Speak kindly so that we can feel encouraged.
Speak tenderly so that we will feel loved.
Speak to us through your words God,
read and reflected upon today. Amen.

## We Come with Our Gifts (Offering Dedication)

God who we know as Father, Son and Spirit,
God who we experience as great creator,
loving provider, and giver of all good gifts,
God who calls us children and disciples,
we come with our gifts, a small portion
of the abundance you have blessed us with.
Loving God take these our offerings
that express our love and gratitude
and use them to spread the gospel of love
to the lives our lives touch upon. Amen.

## We are Committed to Living Our Lives for You (Offering Dedication)

God, we are committed to living our lives for you,
giving of our time and talents for you,
giving of our substance to you.
May these offerings we give to you
further the mission you have us do.
We thank you for all you give to us.
Bless the little we give back to you. Amen.

## For Us and For Others (Offering Dedication)

Lord God, we praise and thank you for
all you have done for us and for others,
all that you are doing for us and for others,
all that you have planned for us and for others.
We ask that you bless these gifts given by us for others.
We ask that they accomplish your work in your world
of bringing faith, hope and love to others as to us;
and we praise and thank you for your generosity
that has enabled us to bring these gifts,
and for your compassion towards us
and towards others. Amen.

## In Worship of the God who Loves (Offering Dedication)

*1 John 4:7-12*

In worship of the God who loves,
we bring gifts because we love,
to the church begun in love,
to do the work of the Lord of love.

Holy One, the God who loves,
bless these offerings we bring in love
to fund the church's work of love,
in a world much in need of love. Amen.

## Our Small Gifts (Offering Dedication)

*John 6:4-14, 27*

Jesus who took a small gift
of five little loaves and two fish
and with it fed a large crowd,
take these small gifts we bring
and with them feed a multitude
with more than perishable food.
Add to these gifts your holy gift
of bread that endures for eternal life.
Bring love and hope, joy and peace
through these small gifts we bring.
Grant blessings to the folk who give
and to those who will receive, and
when these gifts have been consumed
may what remains be so much greater
than these gifts we now dedicate
for the work of your church. Amen.

## Your Gift of Wisdom (Intercession)

Lord, every day people in authority
make decisions on our behalf.
We pray that they make wise decisions
that are beneficial not detrimental.
We know the sage spoke truly when he said,
"when the godly are in authority the people rejoice,
but when the wicked are in power, they moan."
We pray for those in authority,
that their decision making will be for good and not for ill.
**We pray for your gift of wisdom for them and for ourselves.**

Lord, we pray that those meeting in cabinet rooms
will make beneficial decisions,
that those meeting in council chambers
will make well-informed decisions,
that those meeting in boardrooms
will make ethical decisions,
and that those meeting in court rooms
will make astute decisions.
We pray that their decision making
will be for good and not for ill.
**We pray for your gift of wisdom for them and for ourselves.**

Lord, we pray that those working within schools
will make insightful decisions,
that those working within hospitals
will make perceptive decisions,
that those working within government departments
will make helpful decisions,
and that those working within prisons
will make discerning decisions.
We pray that their decision making
will be for good and not for ill.
**We pray for your gift of wisdom for them and for ourselves.**

Lord, we pray that those serving on parish councils
will make visionary decisions,
that those serving on church committees
will make careful decisions,
that those serving as pastors and church administrators
will make caring decisions,
and that those serving in charities and NGOs
will make prudent decisions.
We pray that their decision making
will be for good and not for ill.
**We pray for your gift of wisdom for them and for ourselves.**

Lord, we pray that all those involved
in making far reaching decisions,
will first consider the effects
their decisions will have on others,
particularly upon the poor and the powerless.
We ask that you give them
the insight and wisdom to ensure
that their decision making will be for good and not for ill.
**We pray for your gift of wisdom for them and for ourselves.**

We thank you for hearing our prayer. Amen.

## Living in a Pain filled World (Intercession)

*Luke 21:9-11*

Sovereign God we live in a pain filled world;
a suffering world where
bombs fall and innocent children die;
a suffering world where
a murderous white supremacist
shoots peaceful people at prayer;
a suffering world where
a new disease sweeps round the world
causing distress and killing the vulnerable.

Sovereign God, we live in a pain filled world,
so help us elect leaders of compassion
who don't retaliate bombings by dropping more bombs.
Help us create communities of welcoming people
who embrace not exclude folk
of different faiths and traditions.
Help us become a knowledgeable people
able to limit the spread of panic and pandemics.

Sovereign God we live in a pain filled world,
but we have the hope that comes from knowing
that you are faithful and always with us.
Giving us strength in times of testing
and never letting us be tested beyond our endurance.
Giving us hope in troubling times
and never letting us fall into despair.
Giving us joy even when sorrow threatens to rob us of laughter
and filling us with your light when the world seems very dark.

Sovereign God, we live in a pain filled world.
Be with the people in war torn regions of this world.
Protect them and bring them the peace they crave.
Be with the people persecuted because of their race or religion.
Protect them and bring them the peace they crave.
Be with the people suffering from or living in fear of illness.
Protect them and bring them the peace they crave.
Sovereign God, hear our prayer for this pain filled world. Amen.

**Loving God, Where there is...** (Intercession)

Loving God,
Where there is drought send gentle and sustained rain.
Where there is flooding send away the storm clouds
and cause rainbows to break through.
Where waterways are polluted and lakes are toxic bring restoration.

**Gracious God we thank you for the water of life
and we pray for those who have too little water
or are inundated with too much water,
or have access only to water that brings death not promotes life.**

Loving God,
Where there is misunderstanding between peoples bring discernment.
Where there are cultural differences between peoples bring acceptance,
so that ethnic diversity become a cause for celebration.
Where there is violence bring peacefulness.

**Gracious God we thank you for all the peoples of the earth
with all their customs and creeds and cultures.
We pray for people caught up in places of conflict,
victims of the political agendas of men and women
for whom the bomb not the ballot box
is the way to power and influence.**

Loving God,
Where there is illness bring helping hands.
Where there is sadness bring healing words
that transform tears of sorrow into tears of laughter.
Where there is death bring the hope of life eternal.

**Gracious God we thank you for all health workers and home helpers
who work to make the sick well and the infirm comfortable.
We pray for all those who struggle with depression,
for those feeling hurt and betrayed, and for those who mourn.**

Loving God we pray for your presence in the world.
**Gracious God we pray for your deliverance of the world.**

Loving God we pray for your transformation of the world.
**Gracious God we pray that your life affirming Spirit will flow
through the lives of all people and creatures on earth. Amen.**

## Your Great Love (Intercession)

*Mark 5:21-43*

We pray for children who are seriously ill
who are not only suffering from their sickness
but because of their young age aren't asked
for input into decisions on their medical treatment.

**God we ask you to comfort these children.**
**Support them and encourage them every day.**
**During their suffering be there beside them.**
**May they perceive your great love for them.**

We pray for the parents of very ill children
worrying about what is best for their child,
fervently hoping that their child will recover
even when the prognosis says otherwise.

**God we ask you to comfort these parents.**
**Support them and encourage them every day.**
**During their distress be there beside them.**
**May they perceive your great love for them.**

We pray for the people who are getting sicker,
seeking in vain for a treatment to cure them,
distressed by knowing they are getting weaker,
hoping for a medicine that will really work.

**God we ask you to comfort these patients.**
**Support them and encourage them every day.**
**During their affliction be there beside them.**
**May they perceive your great love for them.**

We pray for the people who have a disability,
for whom everyday life is an everyday struggle.
Tasks that are easy for an able bodied person
require a huge effort for the disabled to do.

**God we ask you to comfort the disabled.**
**Support them and encourage them every day.**
**During their challenges be there beside them.**
**May they perceive your great love for them. Amen.**

## The God who runs towards you (Commissioning)

*Luke 15:11-32; Romans 8:29; Hebrews 4:14-16; John 16:13-15*

Go out from here into the world
with the assurance that comes from knowing
that nothing can diminish God's love for you,
for you are a child cherished beyond measure,
whom God is delighted to share creation with.
Turn towards God, and God will run towards you,
and will be for you a generous, loving parent,
an understanding, compassionate first born sibling,
and a constant companion who will be your guide in life
when you are close to your spiritual home
and when you travel far away. Amen.

## The Beloved of God (Blessing)

You are the beloved of the life-giving Father,
the cherished of the resurrected Son,
and the comforted of the advocating Spirit.
May you be blessed throughout the week ahead,
experiencing the loving presence of God –
who is Father, Son and Spirit. Amen.

## Courageous Faith (Blessing)

God bless you with courageous faith.
Faith that moves the mountains in your lives.
Faith that crosses the Red Seas in your lives.
Faith that enables you to go forth and face
the challenges of life confidently, knowing you will prevail.
God bless you with a strongly convicted faith. Amen.

**Remember How Much God Loves You** (Meditation)

*Lamentations 3:22-26*

When you face considerable obstacles and feel discouraged,
be encouraged by remembering how much God loves you.
When you face hurtful discrimination and feel marginalised,
be encouraged by remembering how much God loves you.
When you face an uncertain future and feel very afraid,
be encouraged by remembering how much God loves you.
Even in times of trouble have confidence in the Lord,
for God's faithfulness is great, and his mercies never end.
Remember God's grace rises with you every morning,
and wraps snugly around you when you lie down at night.
So with hope wait quietly for God's deliverance, and always
be encouraged by remembering how much God loves you. Amen.

# *Creation Day*

## All Creation Praises You (Opening/Gathering)

*1 Chronicles 16:28-34; Isaiah 55:12; Psalm 99:4-9*

All creation comes before you to praise you.
Singing and barking, chirping and mewing.
**All creation comes before you to praise you,**
**a celebratory gathering of all living beings.**

All creation comes before you to praise you.
Swaying and swimming, flapping and spinning.
**All creation comes before you to praise you,**
**dancing to music with a celestial rhythm.**

All creation comes before you to praise you.
Clapping hands and flippers, paws and wings.
**All creation comes before you to praise you,**
**revering with joy the God of all living things.**

All creation comes before you to praise you.
Earth is a holy sanctuary spinning in space.
**All creation comes before you to praise you,**
**for everything on earth receives your grace. Amen.**

## We Gaze in Wonder at Creation (Praise/Thanksgiving)

*Genesis 1:1-28; 2 Peter 3:8; Psalm 90:4*

God we gaze out in wonder
into the vastness of the endless universe,
at the billions of spiralling galaxies
each consisting of billions of burning stars;
and we ponder what it means to say
you brought all this into being by saying,
"Let there be light."

God we gaze up in wonder
at the blue sky across which white clouds drift,
and we look out at the sea delighting in
its blue waters and white foaming surf;
and we ponder what it means to say
you brought all this into being by saying,
"Let there be an atmosphere and water on the earth."

God we gaze around us in wonder
at majestic mountains and wide open plains.
We delight in the variety of flora and fauna
that occupies every environment on earth;
and we ponder what it means to say
you brought all this into being by saying,
"Let life begin to develop on the earth."

God we gaze back in time in wonder
at what fossilised remains reveal to us
about how the earth was eons ago,
when the whole planet was lush with vegetation
and great creatures ruled over land, sea and sky;
and we ponder what it means to say
that for you a thousand years is like a day.

God we gaze with interest on human artefacts
dug up by archaeologists that clearly show
humans have always had a sense of the divine,
that worship appears built into our DNA;
and we ponder what it means to say
you brought humanity into being by saying,
"Let us make humankind in our image,
and give them dominion on the earth."

God we gaze in wonder at your creation
and join with the cosmos in giving praise. Amen.

## A Better Understanding (Illumination)

*1 Chronicles 16:31-33; Romans 8:20-21; Psalm 89:11;*
*Genesis 1:27-28, 2:15*

In scripture we read that all the earth
trembles before the holy splendour of God;
that seas, fields and forests express great joy
that God is coming to justly judge the earth.
For the creation itself longs to be set free
from bondage to unrelenting decline and decay.

God help us remember that we too are
just a part of a global ecological system,
and don't have permission to exploit and destroy,
but rather we are called to be faithful curators,
nurturing the earth and its many life forms,
helping all things flourish in their assigned place.

God to you belong everything you created,
the vast heavens and the beautiful earth.
God through your scriptures bring us to
a better understanding of our responsibilities
as the species you made to be somewhat like you,
and to whom you entrusted dominion over your earth. Amen.

## The Giver of All We Claim to Own (Offering Dedication)

*Psalm 24:1, 50:9-11; Matthew 6:26, 25:40; Acts 20:35*

God who owns all the wild animals of the forest,
God to whom belong all that moves in the fields,
God who knows all the birds that fly through the air,
what can we bring to you that isn't yours already?

Just as you provide seeds for the cheeky sparrow
and krill and small fish for the humpback whale,
so you are the giver of all that we claim to own,
the proprietor of the earth from which our wealth comes.

God you have given us the privilege of participating
in your work of redemption and reconciliation.
God you have given us the opportunity of contributing
our offerings to help fund your work in this place.

Having richly blessed us we ask you to bless others
through the gifts we bring for the work of the church.
We know that there are blessings to be had in giving
and that in serving others we are serving you. Amen.

## All Things are Being Reconciled (Commissioning)

*2 Corinthians 5:17-21; Matthew 28:20; Isaiah 65:17; Revelation 21:1-2*

With Christ, God began a new world order,
in which all things are being reconciled to God.
Humanity no longer needs to be estranged
from God the Creator and from God's creation.

You are commissioned to be Christ's envoys
to whom is entrusted this message of hope.
Fulfil your God-given assignment in the world
by showing your love for God and God's creation.

As you go out know that God goes with you,
and will always be close until the end of the age,
when the renewing of creation will be completed,
and God will reveal a new heaven and earth. Amen.

# *Spring Flower Sunday*

## The Warming of the Air and the Flowering of the Earth
(Praise and Confession)

The warming of the air and the flowering of the earth
tells us that spring has come once more –
a time of great beauty and a time of growing hope
for the abundance to be harvested in the coming autumn.

The warming of our souls and the flowering of our praise
shows us that the Spirit is working in our lives –
growing our faithfulness, inspiring loving kindness
helping us live our lives in spiritual abundance.

But the feel of winter clings on in the chill of the winds
that blow over mountains still covered in snow,
and spring showers fall when grey clouds accumulate
blocking from the earth the full light and warmth of the sun.

And we confess that at times we cling onto old attitudes and habits
far too long
and are deaf to your call to embrace new ideas and new ways of being.
We confess that often we aren't as attuned to your Spirit as we should be
and end up blocking the full strength of your radiance in our lives.

Gracious God you have been with us in all the seasons of our lives;
in seasons of plenty and of joy and in seasons of struggle and sorrow,
in seasons of beauty and growth and in seasons of unsightliness
and decline,
in seasons when we delight in You and in seasons when we ignore You.

Gracious God as life bursts out on the earth anew this springtime
may your Spirit burst forth anew in our lives and in the church,
filling our minds with wonder, our hearts will gratitude,
our souls with joy, and our lips with praise of you. Amen.

**Flowers in the Garden of God** (Blessing)

You are flowers in the garden of God,
each individually precious,
and together truly beautiful,
the children of a loving Father,
the disciples of a caring Lord.
Go from here knowing that
you have been made fragrant
by the life of Jesus, and
lovely by the presence of the Holy Spirit.
Go from here knowing that
the love of God is always with you
and with all who are important to you. Amen.

# *Blessing of the Animals*

## Treasuring All Living Species (Praise/Thanksgiving)

There are animals we share our homes with
and animals that we go into the wild to see.
Animals that contribute to our well-being
and animals that are vital to our economy.

There are animals whose antics make us smile
and animals whose presence we enjoy.
There are animals who we are afraid of
and animals we rely on to keep us safe.

God we thank you for the vision of seeing-eye dogs
who give the blind freedom to move around.
God we thank you for the noses of sniffer dogs
who identify substances and pests we need to find.

God bless the animals we have brought before you,
our pets who are loved members of our families.
Bless every crawling, running, swimming, flying creature,
those who live near us and those who live far away.

Every species has arisen from your creativity,
every animal is a testament to your brilliance.
Give us a heart to treasure every living species,
the creatures we share this planet with. Amen.

## Bless the Creatures of Field and Sky (Blessing)

*Genesis 2:18-20*

God an ancient narrative tells of you making
living creatures from the ground to be companions
for the earth man Adam who you had formed.
Although Adam did not find a partner to help him
from among all the creatures of field and sky,
humanity has always lived in close proximity to animals.
In many ways our lives have depended on them.
What you brought to Adam we now bring to you,
seeking your blessing on the creatures Adam named.
Bless the animals of the fields and the birds of the sky
and may we earthlings live more in harmony with them. Amen.

## God Bless Your Pets (Blessing)

*Revelation 4:7-8*

May the God at whose throne are living creatures,
resembling a lion, an ox, a human being and an eagle,
bless the animals you have brought into your life,
the animals who look to you for sustenance and love.
May you long enjoy the company of your pets,
and may they enjoy sharing their lives with you.
God bless your pets and God bless you. Amen.

## Predator Free Aotearoa/New Zealand (Meditation)

*Isaiah 11:6-9*

God we are facing the consequences of past actions.
Our ancestors brought with them foreign species;
predators that now feed on native birds and animals
causing them to decline to the brink of extinction;
herbivores that veraciously consume native flora
and weeds that crowd out indigenous plants.
The natural balance between flora and fauna
that was in Aotearoa before we humans arrived
has been compromised in most of the country.

There are no good or bad animals or plants.
Each living thing does what it was designed to do.
Only when taken outside its original environment
does an animal or plant threaten indigenous species,
and cause native habitats to begin to decline.
We have embarked upon the eradication of pests
which involves the cruelty of wholesale slaughter.
We remember life depends on death, a cycle of
eating and being eaten is what you brought into being.

But like the prophets of old we find this disturbing.
They dreamed of a differently ordered world
in which wolf and lamb could live peacefully together,
and the cow and the bear would both feed on straw.
But that world only exists in prophetic imagination,
so we go forth with our traps and poisoned bait
to eliminate problem species with prodigious appetites.
Help us in this effort to help restore the natural balance
that we humans disturbed, beginning centuries ago. Amen.

# *All Saints Day*

## The Relay Race of Faith (Candle lighting)

*Hebrews 12:1*

We light this candle in remembrance
of those who have gone before us.
**We remember the cloud of witnesses
who have completed their race of life.**

We light this candle in acknowledgement
of the saints who are here with us.
**We encourage one another to run with perseverance
this race set before us.**

We light this candle in celebration
of the saints who will come after us.
**We cheer on the runners
to whom we are passing on the baton of faith.**

We light this candle in thanksgiving
for all saints, past, present and future.
**We give thanks for victories won,
and hope for victories yet to come. Amen.**

## God Spoke in Various Ways (Illumination)

*Hebrews 1:1-2*

In the past God you spoke in many
and various ways through
the stories of the sages,
the instructions of lawgivers,
the warnings of prophets,
the proverbs of philosophers,
and the psalms of the poets.

Now you speak directly to us by your Son;
but to hear his voice we still need to read
these ancient texts as interpreted by
the Jesus-focused authors of the gospels
and the writers of exhortatory letters
to the first generation of Christian saints.

Without your help God we cannot
fully comprehend these sacred writings
or truly perceive their relevance for us.
We ask you to open our minds to all
you would have us learn through the
reading and preaching on scripture today. Amen.

## In the Shadow of the Saints (Intercession)

*Matthew 15:31-46*

Great God we stand in the shadow
of the saints who have gone ahead of us;
the saints who down through the ages
have lived according to your word.

The saints who gave food to the hungry
and were always hospitable to strangers.
The saints who gave clothes to the needy
and sought to improve the lives of prisoners.

The saints who struggled to end slavery
and championed the poor and distressed.
The saints who took care of the sick
and established the first infirmaries.

Great God we cast our shadows
on the saints who will follow us;
the saints who will be either inspired
or discouraged by the example we set.

May we answer your call to take good care
of the people who can't care for themselves.
May we answer your call to speak up boldly
for the people without a voice of their own.

May we answer your call to be welcoming
to the foreigners and refugees among us.
May we make sacrifices for justice and peace
wherever people are being treated unfairly.

Great God bless the parade of saints
who down through the ages have heard
the cry of the poor and the distressed
and have responded by doing your work. Amen.

## Among the Saints (Blessing)

*1 Corinthians 1:1-3; 2 Thessalonians 3:16; Hebrews 12:22-24*

You are the beloved of God.
At this time and in this place
you are among those chosen
and sanctified by God, to be
among the saints who come
before the throne of heaven.
To you and to all the saints
who call upon the name of Jesus,
be the grace of God and
the peace that Jesus gives
at all times and in all ways
to all who faithfully follow him. Amen.

# *Reign of Christ Sunday*

## We have Come to Worship the Holy One (Opening/Gathering)

*Matthew 1:23; 16:16; John 1:1-3, 49-51, 10:11; Hebrews 3:1;*
*1 Corinthians 15:45; Revelation 5:12-13, 17:14, 21:23, 22:16*

We have come to worship the Holy One,
Emmanuel, the always with us God.
**We have come to worship the Holy One,**
**the Logos who spoke creation into being.**

We come to worship the Holy One,
the apostle and high priest of God.
**We have come to worship the Holy One,**
**the last Adam, the life-giving spirit.**

We have come to worship the Holy One,
the sacred sacrifice, the Lamb of God.
**We have come to worship the Holy One,**
**the good shepherd who laid down his life for his sheep.**

We have come to worship the Holy One,
the Messiah, the chosen one of God.
**We have come to worship the Holy One,**
**the root and branch of David.**

We come to worship the Holy One,
the lamp for the light of God.
**We have come to worship the Holy One,**
**the King of Kings, and Lord of Lords.**

We have come to worship the Holy One,
the Son of Man and Son of God.
**We have come to worship the Holy One.**
**We have come to worship Jesus. Amen.**

### King Jesus Giver of All Good Gifts (Offering Dedication)

King Jesus, giver of all good gifts
**receive from us our gifts to you;**

small gifts to grow your realm of love,
**small gifts that express our love for you.**

King Jesus, bless the gifts we give.
**Use them for your work of grace.**

Bless others through the gifts we give.
**Bless us in the giving too. Amen.**

### The King Whose Throne was a Cross (Blessing)

May the King who was enthroned upon a cross,
who was crowned with a wreath of thorns,
reign supreme in your lives;
constantly pouring out the love
and administering the mercy
of God on your behalf;
and may the royal presence of our Sovereign Lord,
God who is Father, Son and Spirit,
bestow upon you his bountiful blessings
this day and forevermore. Amen.

### The Sovereign Lord (Commissioning)

*Hebrews 9:11-12*

May the Sovereign Lord,
whose throne was a cross
whose crown was a wreath of thorns,
whose royal robe was a soldier's cloak,
and whose bed chamber was a cold garden tomb,
be the liege lord of your life.

May the Anointed One,
supreme high priest and perfect sacrifice,
who has entered the holy of holies
and now sits at the right hand of God,
reign over you gently, bless you greatly
and guide you daily as you seek to follow him. Amen.

**As Citizens of God's Kingdom** (Commissioning)

As citizens of God's kingdom,
as agents of God's grace,
as believers of God's gospel,
go out into the world,
knowing God's love,
showing God's love,
and growing in God's love.
As you go may you know that God –
Sovereign, Saviour and Spirit –
goes with you, and is with you
wherever you choose to go,
wherever you choose to stay,
and that God intends to bless you
this day and every day throughout
your lifelong pilgrimage. Amen.

# Part 2: Season of Creation

# *Forest Sunday*

## A Tree of Life (Opening/Gathering)

*Proverbs 3:18, 11:30, 13:12, 15:4; Galatians 5:22-23; Hebrews 11:1;*
*1 Kings 19:11-13; Matthew 22:1-14; John 6:57-58*

The Holy Spirit of God is present among us.
**The wisdom of God is a tree of life for us.**

Many are the good fruits the Holy Spirit produces.
**The fruit of righteousness is a tree of life for us.**

The Holy Spirit fills our hearts with hopefulness.
**The assurance of faith is a tree of life for us.**

The Holy Spirit speaks to us softly and gently.
**The Word of God is a tree of life for us.**

The Holy Spirit has set a banquet before us.
**The food God provides is a tree of life for us.**

We have assembled to worship together.
**We have come to eat from God's tree of life. Amen.**

## Grateful for Trees (Thanksgiving)

God we express our appreciation for earth's many trees.
They use our carbon dioxide and give us oxygen in return.
We breathe because of the abundance of trees.
**God we are grateful for trees, for trees sustain life.**

God we express our appreciation for earth's fruiting trees.
They beautify spring with their delicate blossom and in
summer and autumn they provide us with fruit and nuts.
**God we are grateful for trees, for trees sustain life.**

God we express our appreciation for earth's timber trees.
They grow strong and tall through foul weather and fair
and from their sawn timbers we construct our homes.
**God we are grateful for trees, for trees sustain life.**

God we express our appreciation for the earth's forest trees.
They provide food and shelter for the creatures living in them
and a protective canopy for the plants growing beneath them.
**God we are grateful for trees, for trees sustain life.**

God we express our appreciation for earth's soil stabilising trees.
They minimise erosion on hillsides when they grow close together
and when planted in rows they protect ploughed soil from the wind.
**God we are grateful for trees, for trees sustain life.**

God we express our appreciation for earth's rain making trees.
They take moisture from the ground and release it into the air
and raindrops caught by their leaves evaporate making more rain.
**God we are grateful for trees, for trees sustain life.**

God we express our appreciation for all the earth's trees.
We thank you for bringing these wonderful plants into being,
and pray that all humanity will treasure and protect them.
**God we are grateful for trees, for trees sustain life. Amen.**

### As the Wind Rustles Through the Leaves of Trees (Intercession)

As the wind rustles through the leaves of trees
so come Holy Spirit blow through our lives,
not so strongly that we bow and break,
more like the gentle touch of a puff of air.
Cause us to be as responsive to you,
as the leaves that flutter in the slightest breeze.

But if we're indifferent to your gentle persuasion,
if we're too content in our complacency,
then blow a lot harder and if need be
cause us to bend and send our leaves flying.
Crack off the branches that are diseased and dying,
test to see how deeply our roots are embedded.

Holy Spirit give us a passion for your creation,
especially for the forests that are under attack,
from developers wanting to clear land to build on,
from peasants needing firewood to burn,
from diseases finding new species to infect,
from foresters engaged in illegal logging.

Holy Spirit give us a passion for your creation,
the world you began creating eons ago.
Help us kick up a storm of indignant protesting,
when we see big business causing destruction.
Help us find ways to lighten the burden
of indigenous peoples who fell trees to survive.

Holy Spirit give us a passion for your creation.
Grant us success with reforestation.
Help us eradicate diseases and pests.
Assist us save species under threat of extinction.
Holy Spirit blow us into changing our lifestyles,
be the gale that transforms us and our world. Amen.

## Like a Flourishing Forest (Offering Dedication)

A single tree is a truly wonderful plant,
but a forest of trees is a magnificent sight.
One pair of birds will nest within a single tree,
but an eco-system thrives under a forest canopy.
It takes a great many trees to make a great forest
and committed believers to make a great church.
Our achievements are limited when we stand alone.
More is accomplished when we are gathered together.
God we bring you our gifts which we ask you to bless
for the work of the congregation you've planted here.
May your church become like a flourishing forest
that protects and nourishes all seeking its shelter. Amen.

## Be Like a Tree (Commissioning)

*Jeremiah 17:7-8; John 4:10-14; 1 John 4:11-12;*
*Galatians 5:22-23; 1 Peter 4:12-13*

Be like a mighty tree in the forest of God.
Root yourself deeply in the soil of your faith.
Drink often from the Spirit's streams of living water.
Feed yourself regularly on the words of scripture.
Release love into the environment around you.
Provide a covering for those needing shelter.
Produce good fruits for those needing to eat.
Bend but don't break when the storms of life blow.
Flourish free of anxiety in the times of drought.
Resist being burnt up by life's fiery ordeals.
Be a giant tree that others look up to.
Know you are treasured by the forester God. Amen.

## The Spirit is in the Forest (Meditation)

The Spirit is in the forest,
it's her favourite place to play.
She dances in the tops of the trees,
rustles down among the ferns,
sends bird song out on the breeze.

The Spirit is in the forest,
it's her favourite place to play.
She splashes about in the streams,
burrows around in the dark places,
weaves a web of filtered sunbeams.

The Spirit is in the forest,
it's her favourite place to play,
She disturbs the peace like a ruru,[1]
gossips at dawn with the kākā,[2]
swoops between trees like a kererū.[3]

The Spirit is in the forest,
it's her favourite place to play.
She darts about like a pīwakawaka,[4]
slowly crawls around like a giant wētā,[5]
glides at night like a pekapeka.[6]

The Spirit is in the forest,
the gallery displaying her artistry.
It's a habitat she desires we respect,
for she crafted all that lives here,
every tree, every bird, every insect.

The Spirit is in the forest,
the abode that is her delight.
But here she reveals her vulnerability,
for she needs us to care for her playmates,
the creatures under the forest canopy.

---

1 Owl (morepork)
2 Parrot
3 Wood pigeon
4 Fantail
5 Large insect
6 Bat

# *Land Sunday*

## All Creation Joins Us in Worship (Opening/Gathering)

*Genesis: 1:1-31; Psalm 104 & 148*

Aeons ago God you set in motion a process
that led to planet earth and eventually to us.
**All creation joins us in worship of the Creator God.**

You established the earth's elliptical orbit of the sun
at the right distance for the emergence of life.
**All creation joins us in worship of the Creator God.**

You covered the land with luxurious plants,
food for the beasts that wandered the land.
**All creation joins us in worship of the Creator God.**

You brought into being an inquisitive creature
to whom you entrusted the care of the land.
**All creation joins us in worship of the Creator God.**

Today on Land Sunday we praise you for the
land that supports us, the land where we stand.
**All creation joins us in worship of the Creator God. Amen.**

## The Land (Praise)

The land is flat, undulating and steep.
The land has been sculptured by water.
**Glaciers carved out lakes and riverbeds.**

Winds and water eroded the mountains,
and braided rivers formed wide plains.
**Praise God for the land and for its water.**

The land is where we build our homes.
Here we create our local communities.
**The land is where we raise our families.**

Here we acquire our national identity.
The land is the ground on which we walk.
**Praise God for the land and for its people.**

The land is the source of all that grows.
Plants are the source of all that we eat.
**In order to thrive plants need fertile soil.**

Soil consists of four major components:
minerals, organic matter, water and air.
**Praise God for the land and for its soil.**

The land is farmed to grow food for us.
The land is logged to provide us timber.
**The land is mined for the minerals in it.**

The land is quarried for building stone.
The land is drilled for oil and natural gas.
**Praise God for the land and for its resources.**

The land is precious, it's our only home.
It is essential that we truly treasure it.
**The land is vulnerable to being exploited.**

We are responsible for protecting it.
The land is sanctified, it belongs to God.
**Praise God for the land in which God is present. Amen.**

## People of the Land (Confession)

*Matthew 19:26; Philippians 4:13*

We are people of the land.
**We depend on the land's fertility.**

We are people of the rivers.
**We need pure water to drink.**

We are people of the forests.
**We live in houses made of wood.**

We are people of the sky.
**We need both sunshine and rain.**

We are people of the wind.
**We need both warm and cooling breezes.**

We are people of the lakes.
**We use hydro-electricity.**

We are people of the mountains.
**We are inspired by earth's wild places.**

We are people of the Creator God,
caretakers of God's land.
**We are holding the land in trust
for generations yet to come.**

We are people who are sinners.
**We have strayed from our calling.**

We are people who are greedy.
**We have gobbled up earth's resources.**

We are people who are challenged
to put right the wrong we've done.
**We are people who are required
to mend what we have broken.**

We must remove all that contaminates
the land and its veins the waterways.
**We must stop spewing greenhouse gasses
and other pollutants into the air.**

We must restore drained marshlands,
and plant trees to replace felled forests.
**We must do a task too great for us alone,**

but all thing are possible in partnership with God.
**God the Spirit wise and healing guide us
on bringing the land back to health. Amen.**

### Cries from the Ground (Meditation)

*Genesis 4:1-13*

The blood of the creatures now extinct
is crying out to God from the ground,
condemning our destruction of habitat
in our lust for more and more arable land.

A land that once sang loudly with birdsong
is now silent because the forest is gone,
felled and burnt to make pasture land
because there was money in growing sheep.

Nitrogen pollution is the cost we pay
for farming cows on an industrial scale.
Oxygen depleted rivers can't support fish
because we supply cheap milk to the world.

We insist on our right to mine for coal
on a plateau where a unique snail dwells,
and consider we have the right to release
to the air the carbon held within the coal.

The gold in an eighteen carat wedding ring
has generated eighteen tonnes of waste,
and toxic heavy metals can contaminate
the water and land around gold mines.

The sin we must master is lurking around,
the lust that we have for ever more wealth,
no matter how generous the earth is to us,
we want more and more of what she has.

We were called to be our brothers' keepers,
to be guardians of earth's many forms of life.
Instead we have brought about the death
of sibling species we were meant to protect.

Our punishment is more than we can bear.
Unprecedented flooding sweeps soil away.
Droughts kill the grass and our animals die.
New pests and diseases are afflicting our trees.

Not just the survival of vulnerable species,
our own survival depends on us changing.
God hears the cries rising from the ground.
God help us hear them and in response repent. Amen.

# *Wilderness Sunday*

## The Wilderness (Opening/Gathering)

*Genesis 16:7-13; Exodus 3:1-6; 1 Kings 19:11-16;*
*Isaiah 43:19; Jeremiah 2:2; Matthew 3:1-4, 4:1-11*

The wilderness is where people have encounters with God.
**Hagar, Moses and Elijah heard God speak in the wilderness.**

The wilderness is where God makes a path for God's people.
**God guided the Israelites as they wandered the wilderness.**

The wilderness is where people are called to return to God.
**John the Baptist was a voice crying aloud in the wilderness.**

In the wilderness we can find ourselves tested and tempted.
**In the wilderness Jesus resisted and overcame temptation.**

The wilderness is where people seek a spiritual experience.
**The church is assembled to worship the God who seeks us. Amen.**

## Praise for the Wilderness (Praise/Thanksgiving)

Creator God we thank you for the wild places,
the places largely untouched by human activity,
the places where creatures live as you intended,
the places of astonishing beauty and mystery.
**God we praise you for creating the wilderness.**

Creator God we thank you for mountainous places,
the snow covered peaks that reach skyward,
the dense forests that provide animals shelter,
the remote lakes sparkling with crystal clear water.
**God we praise you for creating the wilderness.**

Creator God we thank you for the desert places,
the sands that are constantly moved by the wind,
the creatures adapted to survive the intense heat,
the plants that bloom briefly after occasional rain.
**God we praise you for creating the wilderness.**

Creator God we thank you for the wet places,
the lush rain forests through which rivers flow,
the marshlands frequently inundated with water,
the marine reserves where it's forbidden to fish.
**God we praise you for creating the wilderness.**

Creator God we thank you for the wilderness,
for its spectacular beauty and great solitude,
for its preservation of native plants and creatures,
for its protection of pristine water resources.
**God we praise you for creating the wilderness.**

Creator God we thank you for the wilderness,
for showing us what much the earth was once like,
for showing us what more of the earth could be like,
for showing us what is truly important to treasure.
**God we praise you for creating the wilderness. Amen.**

## Losing the Wilderness (Confession)

God, why is our love for greenhouse gas emitting coal
so great that we would destroy wilderness to mine it?
God, why is our love for greenhouse gas emitting oil
so great that we would destroy wilderness to extract it?
God, why is our love for minerals and rare metals like gold
so great that we would destroy wilderness to obtain them?
God, why is our love for timber from trees in native forests
so great that we would cut down wilderness to acquire it.

God we are not without sustainable energy technologies
to replace the use of environmentally harmful coal and oil.
God we are not without resource recovery technologies
to rescue, recycle and reuse the metal in things thrown away.
God we are not without forests of exotic fast growing trees
to provide the timber we need for our building projects.
So why do we persist in destroying the wilderness
to extract and harvest what we often don't need?

God help people whose livelihood depends on mining
to find work opportunities in more sustainable industries.
God help people whose livelihood depends on burning oil
to find less polluting sources of energy that meets their needs.
God help people whose livelihood depends on sawmilling
to find sustainable sources of timber from fast growing forests.
God help people to become aware of how our daily actions
are contributing to the destruction of wilderness habitat.

God we confess that each one of us is not without blame
when it comes to the reduction of wilderness areas and
the decline and extinction of living things in the wilderness.
Help us become more aware of the actions we can take
to protect the wild places where wonderful species still live.
Forgive us for having been so destructive and wasteful, and
help us to become more aligned with your way of self-sacrifice,
so that we protect the wilderness and its vulnerable species. Amen.

### Spirit God of the Wilderness (Intercession)

Spirit God of the Wilderness we pray for your blessing
on the Department of Conservation people who care
for the plants and the birds, the bats and the insects,
whose natural habitat is the remote wilderness.

Spirit God of the Wilderness we pray for your blessing
on the folk who take care of New Zealand's great walks
and the people who tramp them experiencing the thrill
of being in an environment largely as nature was intended.

Spirit God of the Wilderness we pray for your blessing
on the Search and Rescue People who go out looking
for those who get lost while tramping through the bush
and those who get injured and need to be airlifted out.

Spirit God of the Wilderness we pray for your blessing
on the rural firefighters and the helicopter pilots
who struggle to extinguish the wildfires that threaten
the native forests and tussock lands of the wilderness.

Spirit God of the Wilderness we pray for your blessing
on the photographers and artists who through their
photographs, films, drawings and paintings bring us
images of wild places we never get to see for ourselves.

Spirit God of the Wilderness we pray for your blessing
on all who truly treasure the world's wilderness places.
Bless all who raise their voices in righteous protest
against human activity that threatens the wilderness. Amen.

**Wilderness Wanderings** (Commissioning)

*Amos 2:10*

When you are discouraged and feel as if you are
climbing up crags in a wilderness completely alone;
when you are disheartened and feel as if you are
trudging through barren deserts totally forsaken;
remember that the God who went before Israel
for forty long years during their wilderness journey,
walks beside you each day of your earthly travels.

Take heart and be courageous knowing that whether
you are hiking flat land and making good progress,
or wading in marshland and sinking into the mud;
whether you're slogging uphill or sliding into gullies,
God is with you on your wilderness wanderings and
will bring you to your Promised Land at journey's end. Amen.

# River Sunday

### River of Life (Gathering)

*Psalm 36:8-9, 46:4, 65:9; Genesis 2:10; Ezekiel 47:1-12;*
*Revelation 22:1-2; John 4:14, 7:37-39*

There is a river whose streams
make glad the city of God,
**a river of life that flowed out of Eden**
**to water the Garden;**

a river of life the prophet Ezekiel saw in a vision
flowing from the Messianic temple
**bringing life to the land of Israel**
**and healing to the Dead Sea;**

a river of life the seer John describes
flowing from the throne of God and the Lamb;
**a fountain of delights streaming from a spring**
**gushing up to eternal life;**

a river of living water from which Jesus
invited the Samaritan woman to drink;
**a river of living water from which Jesus**
**invited the thirsty in the temple to drink.**

This river of life is the Spirit of God that
flows through the universe.
**The river of God is full of the water of life,**
**and we come today to drink our full. Amen.**

## The State of Your Rivers (Confession)

Holy Spirit of the heavens, Holy Spirit of the earth,
the state of your rivers reveals the state of our souls.
The stench of sewage in your rivers is easy to smell.
The clogging of waterways with plastic is easy to see.
Organic nitrogen in your streams is easy to measure.
What we don't easily perceive is our own culpability.

Holy Spirit of the heavens, Holy Spirit of the earth,
although we know we need pure water to be healthy,
we continue economic activities harmful to rivers.
Sediment and slash flows downstream after logging,
chemicals used in farming seep into ground water, and
dangerous metals from mining contaminates streams.

Holy Spirit of the heavens, Holy Spirit of the earth,
we need to repent of the harm done to your rivers.
Clearly we are guilty of degrading river water quality,
and of destroying the habitat of river living species,
and of draining rivers through excessive irrigating,
but our most egregious sin is our refusal to change.

Holy Spirit of the heavens, Holy Spirit of the earth,
the state of your rivers reveal the state of our souls.
Your polluted, exploited, depleted, maltreated rivers
are our sacrifices to the idols we choose to worship.
We humans will do whatever is required to make money
but we're reluctant to make sacrifices to save life on earth.

Holy Spirit of the heavens, Holy Spirit of the earth,
Bring us to our senses, and back to worshipping you.
Help everyone see the urgency of changing behaviours
that result in us destroying the health of your rivers, and
bestow upon us needed skills to restore your waterways.
Then pristine rivers might reflect the purity of our souls. Amen.

## Conservation of Precious Rivers and Streams (Intercession)

God we ask you to empower the people who strive to
protect the fish, birds and insects that live in or near rivers.
God we ask you to grant success to the people who work to
protect the volume and purity of water in rivers and streams.
God we ask you to make flourish the native plants being
restored beside watercourses where they once naturally grew.
God we ask you to prosper the farmers who are destocking
their properties to decrease pollution from organic nitrogen.
God we ask you to give success to the businesses that are
reducing fresh water consumption in their manufacturing.
God we ask you to bless everyone who is making a contribution
to the conservation of our precious rivers and streams. Amen.

## Living Water (Blessing)

*John 4:10-15, 7:37-39; Revelation 22:1-2*

God bless you with Living Water,
the free flowing liquid that sustains physical life.
God bless you with Living Water,
the freely given Spirit that maintains eternal life.
God bless you with Living Water,
that flows from Jesus through you to the world.
God bless you with Living Water,
thirst quenching, life giving, plentiful and pure. Amen.

# *Earth Sunday*

## We Light a Candle for the Earth (Candle lighting)

This candle we light acknowledges our dependence on the earth.
**We light a candle for the earth, our common home.**

This candle we light acknowledges our exploitation of the earth.
**We light a candle for the earth, our common home.**

This candle we light acknowledges our pollution of the earth.
**We light a candle for the earth, our common home.**

This candle we light acknowledges our mistreatment of the earth.
**We light a candle for the earth, our common home.**

We light a candle seeking healing for the earth, our common home. Amen.

## Thanksgiving for the Bounty of the Earth (Thanksgiving)

We give thanks for the soil full of minerals and microbes
in which grow the plants that sustain life on earth.
We give thanks for the rain providing the moisture
to keep the soil living and the plants in it growing.
We give thanks for the sunshine providing the energy
to germinate seeds, and for flowering and fruiting.
We give thanks for the land and the food it produces.
**We give thanks for the bounty of the earth.**

We give thanks for the trees that provide welcome shelter,
from prevailing winds that are bitterly cold,
and for trees that give shade when the sun burns upon us
when the winds are gusty and the air stifling hot.
We give thanks for trees of beauty and grandeur,
and for orchards of trees that abundantly feed us
with delicious sweet fruits and nourishing nuts.
**We give thanks for the bounty of the earth**

We give thanks for carrots and cabbages, potatoes and peas
and all the other vegetables that grow in our gardens
both for our table and when intended for market.
We give thanks for fields of gold ripening grain,
for oats and for barley and for wheat and for rye.
We give thanks for all these wonderful grains
providing the ingredients of our daily bread.
**We give thanks for the bounty of the earth.**

We give thanks for the progression of the seasons
each with its challenges and its opportunities.
Most of all we give thanks for the fellowship of those
who accompany us through all our seasons of life.
We give thanks for those who help one another
get through the tough times of worry and stress.
We give thanks for those who know how to celebrate
when the going is good and there's joy to be shared.
**We give thanks for the blessings we share on the earth. Amen.**

### You Love All Your Creation (Confession)

Great Creator Spirit, you love all your creation;
all beetles, bugs, butterflies and birds,
and all other creeping, flying, swimming and running things.

You have given us a duty of care of this planet;
of its air, its land, its waterways and seas,
to use but not exploit, enjoy but not destroy.

Great Creator Spirit we are incredibly destructive beings.
We drain wetlands and cut down forests and plough plains
without thought of the species whose habitats we are destroying.

We dump waste into your rivers, our plastic pollutes your seas.
We are heating your air with greenhouse gases.
We are scarring your land with our mining activities.

For thousands and thousands of years delicate eco-systems have
supported life in perfect balance and wondrous variety,
making earth a planet of abundance and beauty.

Great Creator Spirit we have been voracious exploiters of the earth.
Oblivious to the fragility of the life that supports our life
we give preference to things we make over what you have made.

This living planet is dying because of us.
We and the earth need a miracle, a great miracle.
Not that you clean up our messes but that you clean up us.

Great Creator Spirit the planet needs healing and so do we.
We need to be healed of our greed and stupidity.
We need to be healed of the thinking that prevents us from changing.

Bring us, all of us, of all political and religious persuasions
to repentance and a common commitment
to live in harmony with you and the world you have made. Amen

133

## Prayer of Confession for an Eco-Church (Confession)

God of all living things:
the abundance of life on earth speaks of your generosity,
the beauty of the world speaks of your artistry,
the grandeur of the universe speaks of your majesty.

**How privileged we are to be given dominion over the earth.**
**How inspired we are by the natural wonders of the world.**
**How awestruck we are by the universe being revealed to us.**

God of all living things:
we confess that we have failed to truly treasure the earth,
we confess that we have exploited greedily the world's gifts,
we confess that we have even littered the heavens with space junk.

**We know that we must take better care of earth's ecology.**
**We know that we must conserve the world's resources.**
**We know that we must clean up the pollution we have caused.**

God of all living things:
help your church cherish all of your wonderful creation,
help your church embrace the challenge of sustainable living,
help your church foster environmental action.

**Show us what to do to protect the earth's flora and fauna.**
**Show us how to preserve what we have and reduce what we use.**
**Show us how to slow down climate change and the dangers it poses.**

God of all living things:
we know that there is something wrong with humanity.
We often do know what to do, but we fail to do it,
we often do know what we should not do, yet continue to do it.

**Forgive us, but more than that help us to change,**
**for the sake of all the life forms who share the world with us,**
**for the sake of all people now and all people to come. Amen.**

## For Healing Humanity and the Earth (Offering Dedication)

God our Creator, Our Saviour, Our Advocate,
we bring offerings in worship of you
as a love gift to show our gratitude
for the abundant resources of the earth,
for the wonderful promises of the gospel,
and for the amazing grace you show to us
by mending our brokenness.
We ask you to bless these gifts we bring
from what the earth has provided for us.
May through the work of your church
you bring healing to humanity and to the earth,
by growing your kingdom in this time and place. Amen.

## A Paradise Planet (Commissioning)

*Genesis 2:9, 15; John 1:4, 14:6*

Apart from God we can achieve little.
Together with God we can do much.
The earth is calling for restoration.
We need to be reconciled with the earth.

Go out from here to do great things.
Go from here in partnership with God.
The earth is calling for regeneration.
We need to respond to the earth's urgent cry.

Go out from here to do your part.
Go from here with God at your side.
The earth is calling for refurbishment.
We need to repair the earth's brokenness.

Go out from here to tend God's garden.
Go from here sensing the presence of God.
The earth is your home, a paradise planet,
where you have access to Jesus, the Tree of Life. Amen.

# *Humanity Sunday*

## A Call for Reformation (Confession)

Loving God,
during the Season of Creation your church calls us to consider
the impact of human activity upon the earth and its people.
Sometimes what we are doing collectively is helpful and healing,
often times it is harmful and destructive.
During the Season of Creation our thoughts turn to the people
who are suffering the most from the effects of pollution and climate
change.
We know that those who suffer most are those who own little
and have contributed the least to the warming of the planet.

Loving God,
it is the world's poorest people who drown in the flood waters
of storm surges.
The rich build their mansions on the hills well above the rising water.
It is the world's poorest people who go hungry in times of draught.
The rich have the money to pay the inflated prices for food.
It is the world's poorest people who drink and bathe in polluted water.
The water of the rich is purified, and they swim in pristine pools.
It is the world's poorest people who work the longest hours
for the lowest pay.
The rich enjoy leisure and their wealth increases
through the labour of others.
It is the world's poorest people who are trapped in dangerous situations.
The rich can go anywhere in their private jet planes and ocean going yachts

Loving God,
you call us to be reformed, and we call on you to reform us.
Scriptures show us your heart for the poor and oppressed.
Help us be like you and champion the cause of the poor.
Scriptures tells us that it is more blessed to give than to receive.
Help us to be like you and generously share our resources with the poor.
Scriptures says we must welcome and be a good neighbour to the stranger.
Help us to be like you and treasure all the people on the earth,
no matter their colour, their race or their creed.
Loving God, may your love for us be reflected in our love for others.
May we respond to the cries of the earth and its suffering people. Amen.

## Guardians of the Earth (Confession)

*Psalm 8:3-5*

We are a privileged species,
but that privilege does not extend
to unrestrained exploitation of the earth.
**God forgive our selfishness.**

We are an innovative species,
but that inventiveness does not excuse
us littering the earth with our discarded creations.
**God forgive our wastefulness.**

We are an adventurous species,
but that exploration does not justify
our colonising territory that is not our own.
**God forgive our greediness.**

We are a favoured species,
but that preferential status does not defend
our abuse and depletion of other species.
**God forgive our cruelty.**

We are a redeemed species,
but being forgiven does not permit
us to treat the rest of creation unethically.
**God forgive our arrogance.**

We are a troublesome species,
but being a problem does not mean
we cannot change to become the solution.
**God help us be guardians of the earth. Amen.**

## The Wisdom within Your Holy Scriptures (Illumination)

*2 Timothy 3:16-17; Hebrews 4:12-13; 1 John 3:16-18; Ephesians 2:10*

God we come seeking your blessing
on our contemplation of the wisdom
to be found within your holy scriptures.
As we read and reflect on these sacred texts
give us insight into what you are saying.
Let us not use these ancient words to justify
our existing preferences and prejudices.
Rather help us to embrace the changes
that your cutting words demand we make.
Help us start caring for your creation
and relieving the distress of the poor. Amen.

## Help Us Become Servant Leaders (Intercession)

*Mark 10:41-45; Genesis 1:26-28; Philippians 2:1-8; Psalm 8:3-8*

God, Jesus was an outstanding leader
who came to serve not to be served,
and to give his life as a ransom for many.
**God help us become servant leaders.**

God, you gave humankind dominion
over all the other species on earth,
to care for creation not dominate it.
**God help us become servant leaders.**

God, Jesus did not exploit his great power
but humbled himself like a lowly slave
and surrendered his life on a cross.
**God help us become servant leaders.**

God, the expertise you have given humanity
is not for our own glory and satisfaction
but to protect the other life forms on earth.
**God help us become servant leaders.**

God help us to realise that our humanity
cannot be a little lower than your divinity
unless we are servant leaders like Jesus.
**God help us become servant leaders. Amen.**

**Transformation** (Commissioning)

*Genesis 2:15; Isaiah 55:12*

Transformation happens when
a great change in perspective motivates
many small changes in human behaviour.
From the start of the industrial revolution
to the modern age of the computer,
we humans have viewed the existence
of the earth as being mainly for our benefit.
Now we must view the purpose of our existence
as being mainly for the care of the earth.
Go out into the world to make a difference,
knowing that God desires you to succeed.
Go out in joy with the blessing of the Creator
and with the acclamation of the earth. Amen.

# *Sky Sunday*

## The Earth and the Sky Declare God's Majesty (Opening/Gathering)

*Psalm 8:1*

We gather on the earth and beneath the sky
**to worship the God who created all things.**

The earth and the sky declare God's majesty,
**and with all creation we proclaim God's glory.**

We worship with the birds that fly in the sky,
**and with the animals that walk on the land.**

The earth where we live is a sanctuary in space.
**The sky is a mantle spread around the earth.**

As we express our gratitude for the sky today,
**God bless our worship with nature we pray. Amen.**

## Praise for the Sky (Praise)

*1 Chronicles 16:29-34; Isaiah 44:23*

God we praise you for the beauty of the sky;
its blue colours that boost up our spirits,
its warm colours that start and end our days,
the sunshine that makes our life possible,
the fluffy white clouds that billow up,
the multi-coloured bow that follows the rain.

God we praise you for the birds of the sky;
the high soaring birds riding the thermals,
the birds that travel together in formation
and the flocks constantly changing direction,
the birds the swoop from tree top to tree top,
and the birds who fly much nearer the ground.

God we praise you for the night time sky;
the moon reflecting the light of the sun,
the uncountable stars shinning from afar,
the Crux constellation we call Southern Cross,
the Aurora Australis glowing in the south,
the streak of light of the meteorite.

God we praise you for all creation
and with all creation we worship you;
with the high mountains that pierce the clouds,
the sea that appears to merge with the sky,
with the winged creatures that fly through the air,
and the trees growing towards the sky. Amen.

## Sky Glow (Meditation)

God we have built our cities on such grand scales
that we've become disconnected from your creation.
Our communities have become so large that although
we live close together we don't know one another,
and so we flood streets and yards with artificial light
to protect ourselves from folk with criminal intent.

We are consuming energy in increasing amounts
to turn night's darkness into an artificial daylight.
So now sky glow keeps us from seeing your stars,
and to view the brilliance laid out in your heavens
we are forced to travel to dark sky reservations,
where with awe we gaze upwards at your creation.

Not just humans live in the cities we have created.
We share our backyards with a variety of species.
Creatures that you designed to hunt in the darkness
now find their strategies are being foiled by our light.
The natural relationships between predator and prey
are being disturbed by us turning night into day.

Like other species that sleep during the night
we need darkness to stimulate enough melatonin.
The negative impact of lost sleep on our health
is now better known and a cause for concern.
But at least we can pull blinds and draw our drapes,
unlike other species that can't shut out our light.

God there are things that we are able to do,
like shield our street lights to reduce light scatter,
install lighting only where it is truly needed,
and use bulbs that produce only the light required,
keep our lighting from disturbing our neighbours,
and eliminate the danger of lighting that glares.

God this generation must change our way of living.
Change is resisted because it can seem to be hard.
But the joy of gazing skyward and seeing the heavens
is surely an incentive to reduce our light pollution.
No matter how challenging, God help us find a way
to restore to our lives the rhythm of night and day. Amen.

## A Glimpse of Your Majesty (Meditation)

*Psalm 19:1-6; Philippians 2:5-11; Genesis 1:27*

All things on earth came from the earth,
and the earth is an offspring of the stars.
The stars brought light to the darkness,
when God spoke the universe into being.

We rely on the sun for light and warmth,
itself made from the debris of the big bang.
Our days are marked by it rising and setting
as our spinning globe orbits its nearest star.

Thousands of millions of other stars form
the galaxy to which our solar system belongs,
all orbiting around a massive black hole,
with many having planets orbiting them.

The Milky Way Galaxy is one of at least
two trillion galaxies in the vast universe.
Such space and power is incomprehensible.
How can we perceive the God that made this!

Long ago a poet wrote how the stars silently
speak of God's glory throughout the world.
What that poet saw was just a small fraction
of the magnificent cosmos now revealed to us.

God's power is greater than we can imagine,
which makes God's mercy truly astonishing.
How audacious to say we're made in God's image
considering how little and fragile we are?

When the early church sang about Jesus
humbling himself to take on human form,
and being obedient even to death on a cross,
how little they knew of the humility entailed.

God you have given us an irrepressible curiosity
that allows us to get glimpses of your majesty,
and by seeing the enormity of your creation
we realise how honoured we are to be loved.

## Day and Night (Meditation)

*Genesis 1:6-8, 14-19*

The dark of night gives way to yellows and reds
as light from the sun begins painting the sky,
announcing its coming before fully emerging
from the sky beneath the eastern horizon.

Bird song greeting the warm colours of dawn
calls us to rise from our night time slumbers.
Light's shortest wavelengths turn the sky blue
as the revolving earth turns us towards the sun.

The ancient world believed the world was flat
and was protected under a dome called the sky.
An ancient poet said God made two great lights,
the greater to rule the day the lesser the night.

God placed these lights in the dome of the sky
and said they'd measure the passing of time,
in days and in months, in seasons and years;
and God saw that what he had made was good.

Fundamentalists and atheists have in common
an insistence on reading the scriptures literally.
The rest of us see an eternal truth in the poetry
that does not require us to embrace fantasy.

God's revelations did not end two millennia ago.
Scientists and astronomers are our modern sages
publishing new facts about God's universe,
confirming God's creation is indeed very good.

The golden light of the late afternoon precedes
the sun sinking beneath the western horizon.
Our place on the planet is now turning away
from the rays of the sun as we enter the night.

# *Mountain Sunday*

## The Spirit of God Blows Over the Mountains (Opening/Gathering)

*John 3:8, 7:37-39*

The Spirit of God blows over the mountains.
**The Spirit like the wind blows all around us.**

The Spirit of God flows down mountain streams.
**The Spirit like water flows through us and from us.**

The Spirit of God snows the mountain peaks white.
**The Spirit like snow covers us with God's love.**

With the majestic mountains reaching skyward
**and the stretched out plains reaching seaward,**

with all the creatures that live in the mountains
**and with all the animals that inhabit the plains,**

we worship the God who brings into being all things.
**We worship the Spirit of God who is everywhere. Amen.**

## Mountains (Opening/Gathering)

*Psalm 36:5-6*

Powerful forces make you,
spewing you up from the hot underworld,
pushing you skywards by tectonic plates colliding.

**Wind and snow define you,**
**reducing your height through erosion,**
**softening your jaggedness with a white frosting.**

Sun and moon reveal you,
making you a mosaic of sunny and shade,
giving you an eerie silhouette in reflected light.

**Forests and flowers dress you,**
**covering your lower slopes with dense vegetation,**
**growing in rocky places above the bush line.**

Creatures enliven you,
piercing your air with the cry of the kea,
climbing your slopes like the sure footed tahr.

**Mystery surrounds you.**
**Gods were once thought to live on you.**
**Few are the people who get to climb you.**

Mountains with you we worship the Creator,
whose righteousness, the psalmist says.
is like the mighty mountains.

**Mountains with you we worship the Saviour,**
**whose love extends far beyond you to the heavens,**
**who protects humans and animals alike. Amen.**

## We Thank You for the Mountains of Aotearoa
(Thanksgiving/Confession)

**God we thank you for the mountains of Aotearoa.**
We thank you for the snow that falls on them,
melting to fill lakes in the high country,
that in turn feed rivers rolling to the sea.
Although from afar the mountains in winter
appear as white as they have always done,
yet a reduced amount of snow is falling on them,
glaciers are shrinking and lakes are low.
Help us to address the causes of global warming
for the sake of the mountains and their snow.

**God we thank you for the mountains of Aotearoa.**
We thank you for the plants that grow on them,
the forests that cover their lower slopes,
the daisies, buttercups, and eyebrights that flower,
where the trees give way to snow tussock grassland,
and the vegetable sheep, lichens and mosses
found further up still among the rocks.
Such high altitude plants are being reduced
by the deer and the tahr we have introduced,
and by invasive weeds that compete for their space.

**God we thank you for the mountains of Aotearoa.**
We thank you for the animals that live in them,
the rock wren that lives above the bush line,
the inquisitive kea the bane of mountain visitors,
the skinks and the geckos the blend in with the rocks,
the giant carnivorous snails in need of more rain,
the oversized weta, the large flightless grasshopper,
the small black cicada, and the black ringlet butterfly.
These unique creatures are being threatened
by introduced predators and the destruction of habitat.

**God we thank you for the mountains of Aotearoa.**
Like elsewhere their biodiversity is being threatened
by the consequences of what we did in the past.
We've cut down the forests destroying eco-systems,
we've mined for and burnt coal releasing its carbon,
we've introduced pests so we could go hunting,
we sent our sheep into the highlands to graze.
Give success to the people working in conservation,
and help foresters and miners find other occupations,
for the sake of the species that live in the mountains.
We confess we have failed to truly value the mountains.
We confess we have failed to protect unique alpine species.
God we acknowledge our errors and ask for your guidance
in reversing the damage we foolishly have done.

**God we thank you for the mountains of Aotearoa. Amen.**

## Go Out to Climb Mountains (Commissioning)

Go out to climb mountains.
Not necessarily Aoraki[7]
or the other peaks of the Southern Alps;
not necessarily Taranaki
or the other volcanoes of Te Ika-a-Māui;[8]
but the mountainous obstacles standing
in the way of returning the earth to being
a healthy home for all living things.

Go out to climb mountains.
If the slopes seem too steep
and the peaks are too high;
look for passes over lower summits
giving access to the side were progress
is occurring to return the earth to being
a healthy home for all living things.

Go out to climb mountains.
With each of us working together,
and with God blessing our efforts,
we can climb over the obstacles
preventing nature recovering
and returning the earth to being
a healthy home for all living things.

Go out to climb mountains,
and in your going know that
with grit and determination,
and with God as our mountain guide,
we will succeed in our endeavour
to help return the earth to being
a healthy home for all living things. Amen.

---

7 Mt Cook
8 North Island

## The Mountain of the Lord (Meditation)

*Exodus 3:19-20; 2 Chronicles 3:1–5:14, 36:17-21; Micah 4: 1-4;*
*Psalm 48:1-8; Matthew 5:1–7:28; Revelation 21:1-17*

God from within a burning bush
you made yourself known
to a disgraced Egyptian prince,
whom you chose to lead your people home.
God in the wilderness of Sin
from the peak of Mount Sinai
you gave the Israelites Torah,
ten commandments to live by.

God on the top of Mount Moriah
in the royal city of Jerusalem
Solomon built for you a temple
and placed your Holy Ark therein.
God that temple was destroyed
and to Babylon the Jews went,
yet they never ceased believing
you would end their punishment.

God they also dared to dream
that the nations would one day say,
"Let's go to the mountain of the Lord
to be instructed in his way."
God that teaching began when Jesus
delivered his sermon on the mount,
when he explained to his disciples
the ethics of the New Covenant.

God for a people who believed
you live on the far side of the sky
Mount Zion is beautiful in elevation
by being near your realm on high.
Here you will build a holy city
to be the joy of all the earth,
here nations will come before you
in the mystical "far north."

God in a vision John saw this city
coming down out of the heavens,
supernatural in its radiance
mountainous in its dimensions.
God this depicts your new creation
where all will live harmoniously.
Here the righteous of the earth
will dwell with you eternally.

# Ocean Sunday

## Spirit of Wisdom (Opening/Gathering)

*Genesis 1:2, 20; Proverbs 8:1, 22-31; Acts 2:1-3*

Spirit of Wisdom who hovered
over the primordial oceans on earth,
erupting up land with explosive fire
bringing the first lifeforms to birth.
**Spirit of God, Spirit of Wisdom**
**we hear you calling to us today.**

Spirit of Wisdom who hovered
over the first Jesus believers on earth,
showing your presence in tongues of fire
bringing the nascent church to birth.
**Spirit of God, Spirit of Wisdom**
**we welcome you here among us today. Amen.**

## Thank You for the Oceans (Thanksgiving)

*Genesis 1:20-21; Psalm 95:5*

Creator God we thank you for the oceans:
for the cooling caress of gentle sea breezes
and the invigorating smell of salt laden air,
for the soothing sound of waves lapping the shore
and the cry of sea birds as they circle above.

Creator God we thank you for the oceans:
for them providing the rain we need in due season,
and for their moderating impact upon the weather,
by cold polar water flowing to the equator
and warm tropical water moving north and south.

Creator God we thank you for the oceans:
for the carbon dioxide absorbing phytoplankton
that produce much of the earth's oxygen,
these tiny organisms help keep us alive
and make animal life possible on the earth.

Creator God we thank you for the oceans:
for all the creatures that make their home in the sea,
for the great whales, the dolphins and porpoises,
for the seals and sea lions, the turtles and sharks,
and for the many species of fish and invertebrates.

Creator God we thank you for the oceans:
for without the oceans we could not be. Amen.

## The Damage We have Done to the Oceans (Confession)

The earth is a jewel spinning in space
in parts sapphire blue with swirls of white,
in parts shot with colour like a costly opal,
but when we look closer we see the damage done
to a once pristine planet now polluted with junk.

**God forgive us for the damage we have done to the oceans**
by dumping plastic waste near rivers and streams,
that is washed into seas and pollutes distant shores
and is mistaken for food by hungry sea birds.
God inspire us to stop dumping all forms of plastic.

**God forgive us for the damage we have done to the oceans**
by using synthetic fertilisers that leach into our rivers
and by allowing effluent to get into the sea
we cause algal blooms that deplete oxygen.
God inspire us to stop using nitrogen and phosphate.

**God forgive us for the damage we have done to the oceans**
by taking too many of the fish species we want
and not avoiding catching the species we don't,
and by destroying the ocean floor by bottom trawling.
God inspire us to establish many more marine reserves.

**God forgive us the damage we have done to the oceans**
by the problems associated with aquaculture,
like the destruction of natural marine habitats,
excess nutrients causing eutrophication,
and diseases transferring from farmed fish to wild.
God inspire us to wisely farm fish sparingly.

**God forgive us the damage we have done to the oceans**
by offshore drilling for oil and natural gas,
the depth of the exploration and wild ocean weather
makes inevitable accidents and oil spills,
which in polluting the oceans destroy wild life.
God inspire us to desist from oil and gas exploration.

**God forgive us the damage we have done to the oceans**
by releasing into the atmosphere stored carbon dioxide
that is absorbed by the sea making it more acidic,
impacting on the ability of shellfish to build shells,
and coral to build skeletons providing shelter for fish.
God inspire us to reduce our release of carbon dioxide.

**God forgive us the damage we have done to the oceans**
and give us the wisdom required to reverse this harm. Amen.

### The Rising Sea (Intercession)

*Job 38:8-11; Proverbs 8:29; Jeremiah 5:2-22*

People praised you God for confining the sea,
before human activity caused polar ice to melt,
glaciers to retreat and warming oceans to rise.
**We pray for the people who are losing
their land and their homes to the rising sea.**

People of the Pacific are in our prayers,
our neighbours whose low lying island nations
are slowly disappearing beneath the waves.
**We pray for the people who are losing
their land and their homes to the rising sea.**

People who live near the sea now fear
storm surges crashing waves over sea walls
and eroding further cliffs by the shore.
**We pray for the people who are losing
their land and their homes to the rising sea.**

People in coastal areas are finding their
fresh water wells are being contaminated
by the salt water of the encroaching sea.
**We pray for the people who are losing
their land and their homes to the rising sea.**

People in seaside communities face the cost
of measures to mitigate the impact of
frequent flooding of increased duration.
**We pray for the people who are losing
their land and their homes to the rising sea.**

People observe the loss of coastal habitat
for creatures that live along the shoreline and
the shrinking of beaches where sea birds nest.
**We pray for the creatures who are losing
their land and their homes to the rising sea.**

People with knowledge remind us that we
are the people responsible for this catastrophe.
God help us make the necessary changes as
**we pray for the people who are losing
their land and their homes to the rising sea. Amen.**

# *Fauna Sunday*

## Creation's Invitation to Worship God (Opening/Gathering)

With birds that chirp and bats that screech
**we worship the creator God.**

With owls that hoot and geese that honk
**we worship the creator God.**

With pigs that squeal and mice that squeak
**we worship the creator God.**

With dogs that bark and sheep that bleat
**we worship the creator God.**

With cows that moo and cats that mew
**we worship the creator God.**

The amazing nature of every creature
testifies to the greatness of their creator,
**and in the sounds each make we hear
creation's invitation to worship God. Amen.**

## Extinction (Confession)

*Genesis 1:28-30*

There once was a time when well out to sea
the sound of bird song could be heard,
but when the forests fell the land went quiet
for the birds who used to sing died out.

God we pray for all the world's creatures
that are categorised as species under threat,
may the desperate interventions underway
help them survive and then to thrive.

Our lust for wealth has cost the planet
a price too high for its life forms to pay,
yet we continue to damage and destroy
the earth's irreplaceable living treasures.

God we pray for all the world's creatures,
that we begin to value them more highly
than what we earn by destroying habitat
or gain by hunting them to extinction.

For the sake of all the endangered species
may all humanity come to understand
that we have dominion over other living things
for their protection not their destruction. Amen.

### For Animal Carers and the Animals Cared For (Intercession)

Spirit of Wisdom we ask you to give wisdom
to the people who share their homes with their pets.
May they provide a happy and healthy environment
in which their pets are loved and well look after.
**We pray for the people who take care of animals
and for the wonderful creatures they take care of.**

Spirit of Wisdom we ask you to give wisdom
to the people who treat hurt and sick animals.
May veterinarians and their assistants be skilled
at relieving the suffering of their animal patients.
**We pray for the people who take care of animals
and for the wonderful creatures they take care of.**

Spirit of Wisdom we ask you to give wisdom
to the people who run animal shelters.
May their loving care undo the harm done
when animals are mistreated or abandoned.
**We pray for the people who take care of animals
and for the wonderful creatures they take care of.**

Spirit of Wisdom we ask you to give wisdom
to the people engaged in conservation projects.
May they be successful in supporting species
whose ongoing existence is under threat.
**We pray for the people who take care of animals
and for the wonderful creatures they take care of.**

Spirit of Wisdom we ask you to give wisdom
to the people who run zoos and wildlife parks.
May they make enclosures replicating the habitats
the animals would have if living in the wild.
**We pray for the people who take care of animals
and for the wonderful creatures they take care of.**

Spirit of Wisdom we ask you to give wisdom
to the people who have animals on their farms.
May they provide ample space for their animals
to live freely and with the minimum of stress.
**We pray for the people who take care of animals
and for the wonderful creatures they take care of.**

Spirit of Wisdom we ask you to give wisdom
to all the people who work with and for animals.
Theirs is the responsibility you gave all humanity
of being the custodians of all creatures on earth.
**We pray for the people who take care of animals
and for the wonderful creatures they take care of. Amen.**

# *Storm Sunday*

## The Strength of the Storm (Praise)

*Exodus 14:21-31; Mark 4:35-40; Genesis 10:11-16; Psalm 107:23-32*

God what words can we use to describe you?
All our words we find totally inadequate.
How can we speak of your immense power
when nothing on earth is as mighty as you?

We know the strength of the storm;
the flashing lightning and the rumbling thunder,
the howling wind that sweeps the sea onto land,
and the roaring sound of a swollen river.

Yet the storm is merely your mechanism
for focussing our attention on you.
You speak and the tempest happens.
You speak and the wind drops away.

God what words can we use to depict you?
All our words we find totally insufficient.
How can we speak of your great authority
when nothing on earth is as powerful as you?

We know the terror caused by the storm;
the sucking tornado and the flattening gale,
the heaving seas that swamp and sink ships,
and the horror of rapidly rising flood waters.

Yet the storm is merely your opportunity
for revealing your incredible mercy,
to remind us on seeing a rainbow
of your covenant with all life on earth.

God what words can we use to define you?
All our words are totally deficient.
How can we speak of your unconditional love,
when nothing on earth loves as greatly as you?

We know the relief after surviving the storm;
the joy when sailors are rescued from drowning,
the compassion of those who assist flood victims,
the hope of those who start to rebuild.

Yet these activities are merely pale reflections
of the salvation you offer to each one of us,
and the grace you give to restore our lives.
So our only words are, "God be praised." Amen.

## Victims of Storms (Intercession)

God we pray for the victims of storms,
for those whose homes are now uninhabitable
having been blown apart by a tornado
or swept away by a swift flowing flood.

God we pray for the victims of storms,
for those whose crops have been destroyed
by soil becoming swamped by excessive rain
or by unseasonable hail stripping off foliage.

God we pray for the victims of storms,
for those whose livestock have been killed
by being drowned in fast rising water
or frozen by a late snow storm in spring.

God we pray for the victims of storms,
for those whose livelihoods have been lost
by strong winds churning up the sea
sinking fishing vessels and destroying ferries.

God we pray for the victims of storms.
Most of all we pray for the bereaved,
those who have lost loved family and friends
who succumbed to the violence of a storm.

God we pray for the victims of storms.
Help us to comfort those who mourn,
help us give the right aid to those in need,
help us to build to withstand future storms.

God climate change is now a reality.
Ferocious storms will be more frequent.
Help us replace talking with taking action
to limit our impact upon earth's atmosphere. Amen.

## Facing the Wind (Blessing)

*Mark 6:35-41; Psalm 107:28-30*

In stressful situations when the future is uncertain,
when the storms of life are overwhelmingly fierce,
God bless you with the faith and the courage you need,
to keep your vessel afloat with you facing the wind.
Know that God is with you in all your circumstances,
when your sails are billowing in a sweet breeze, or
when the waves are so high you fear being swamped.
God accompanies you on your voyage through life
and brings you to a safe harbour when your sailing is done. Amen.

# *Cosmos Sunday*

## Lighting a Candle on Cosmos Sunday (Candle lighting)

On this Cosmos Sunday we light the candle for the earth,
**for its mountains and valleys, its rivers and seas.**

On this Cosmos Sunday we give God thanks for the earth,
**for its beauty that inspires us, its creatures that enthral us,
its abundance that feeds us, its water we drink and
its air that we breathe.**

On this Cosmos Sunday we acknowledge the earth is suffering
**from the effects of global warming, pollution and exploitation.**

On this cosmos Sunday we pray for the earth,
**for the places and people and creatures that are suffering deprivation.
Creator God give us the wisdom to take care of the earth. Amen.**

## Lord of the Universe Beyond Comprehension (Praise)

*Matthew 10:29; Philippians 2:5-8; John 14:7; Genesis 2:1-3, 19:25;
Psalm 136:25; Isaiah 5:16, 44:21-23; Romans 8:18-25*

God who created the vast universe
of trillions of galaxies circling black holes,
we are astonished that you now observe
even the sparrow that falls to the ground.

Lord of the universe beyond comprehension
you rule over all with compassion and care,
we are astonished that you became human
in order to reveal yourself more fully to us.

God who laboured to birth the universe
then rested from all the work you had done,
we are astonished by your unending devotion
to nurturing us and all lifeforms on earth.

Lord of the universe whose righteousness
is apparent through the justice of your judgments,
we are astonished by your willingness to forgive
our abuse of your creation when we repent.

God the master planner, sovereign of all,
who designed the cosmos with eternity in view,
we are astonished you allow creation to groan
while it awaits the revealing of your glory in us.

Lord of the universe, Jesus the Saviour,
God who is intent on redeeming creation,
we are astonished by your unconditional love
and with all creation offer unending praise. Amen.

## God of the Cosmos, Lord of All Living (Confession)

God of the Cosmos, Lord of all living
grant to us the wisdom we urgently need
to take much better care of your creation,
for the suffering earth is crying out to you
as our actions cause her lifeforms to die.

God of the Cosmos, Lord of all living
grant to us the wisdom we urgently need
to stop the terrible harm we are now doing
by not limiting our release of carbon dioxide,
which makes the air hotter, the seas more acidic.

God of the Cosmos, Lord of all living
grant to us the wisdom we urgently need
to clean up the contamination we have caused
to the habitats of our fellow earth creatures,
through our industrial processes that pollute.

God of the Cosmos, Lord of all living
grant to us the wisdom we urgently need
to develop economies that do not require us
to denude the earth through deforestation
or leave her scarred after extracting her wealth.

God of the Cosmos, Lord of all living
grant to us the wisdom we urgently need
to do what humankind has never done before,
to globally change the way we are living
to halt our harmful impact upon the earth. Amen.

**The God who Made the Universe** (Commissioning)

The God who made the universe
and said it was good,
looks down upon you
and says you are good.
Go from here knowing
you are treasured by God.
Go from here knowing
God's infinite love.
The blessings of God
are upon you this day.
The blessings of God
be upon all whom you love. Amen.

# *Climate Sunday*

## Climate Change Deniers (Confession)

God the earth needs you to speak to your people.
They need to know the condition the earth is in.
Together we have caused considerable harm.
Together we can start to repair what we've done.

God too many of us deny that the climate is changing
or rather deny that we are causing this catastrophe.
Bad weather is not unusual so nothing is different,
is the mantra of those who reject climate science.

God our first step towards addressing a problem
is to acknowledge to ourselves the problem exists.
Extreme weather events will impact equally upon
those who accept the science and those who do not.

God too many of us won't make personal sacrifices
to save the earth's eco-systems on which we rely.
We want to continue our resource hungry lifestyles
and dismiss as extremists those calling for change.

God the earth needs you to speak to your people.
They need to acquire quickly a sense of urgency.
They need to understand the crisis we are facing
before it is too late to reverse the damage done.

God too many of us view you as an indulgent parent,
who will put everything right when your Son returns.
Too many of us shirk from our personal responsibility
to change our way of living for the sake of the earth.

God you are a God who brings about transformation.
Our sins are many but the effects of this one is dire.
Help us to collectively repent of our carbon emissions
and inspire us into living a sustainable lifestyle. Amen.

**Crying Out for Deliverance** (Intercession)

We pray
for people in parched lands
longing for rain clouds instead of blue skies.
No moisture for crops to grow,
no water for people to drink.
**People facing starvation are
crying out for deliverance.**

We pray
for people in flooded lands
longing for sunshine instead of stormy skies.
Gentle streams now raging torrents,
avalanches of mud.
**People made homeless by sludge are
crying out for deliverance.**

We pray
for people in wind-blown lands
longing for gentle breezes instead of roaring winds.
Waves whipped up, trees toppled,
roofs blown off, walls blown apart.
**People made homeless by the wind's fury are
crying out for deliverance.**

We pray
for people in shaken lands
longing for stillness instead of earthquakes.
Land thrust up and torn apart,
buildings toppled.
**People trapped under the rubble are
crying out for deliverance.**

We pray
for people in troubled lands
longing for peace instead of violent conflict.
Communities torn apart,
innocence destroyed.
**People seeking safety,
becoming unwanted refugees are
crying out for deliverance.**

We pray
for people in authoritarian lands
longing for freedom instead of repression.
Propaganda masquerading as truth,
civil liberties abolished.
**People in jail for their ideas are**
**crying out for deliverance.**

We recognise
the effects of climate change,
the impact of tectonic forces,
the costs of human violence,
the corruption of unrestrained power,
are filling the world with suffering people.
**The homeless, helpless, persecuted, dispossessed are**
**crying out for deliverance.**

We acknowledge
the problems are too many for us,
the issues are too big for us,
the situations are too complex for us,
the solutions are too far from us.
Nevertheless for the sake of those
crying out for deliverance,
we seek to be people of wisdom
addressing the causes of climate change.
We desire to be people of generosity
meeting the needs of the distressed.
We want to be people of compassion
welcoming the refugees.
**For we are people who pray for those**
**crying out for deliverance. Amen.**

## Climate Champions (Commissioning)

The cumulative impact of the actions of individuals
has brought us to the brink of a climate disaster.
The cumulative impact of the actions of individuals
can create a safety fence on the edge of the cliff.
We are being called to become God's Climate Champions
through the small actions that we can each take.
Like buying only energy efficient appliances
and unplugging equipment when not in use.
Like going by bus, cycling or walking where possible
instead of using our cars for short trips around town.
Like purchasing products that have been made locally
rather than cheaper imported items that aren't as good.
Informing politicians that our votes for them will depend
on their promotion of policies that are good for the earth.
Go out to be God's Climate Champions, remembering that
the cumulative impact of the actions of individuals
can help the earth recover, and by God will be blessed. Amen.

## The Climate is Changing (Meditation)

The climate is changing
and we're beginning to suffer.
In dry places draughts are now lasting much longer,
top soil becomes dust and is blowing away,
grass isn't growing and rivers aren't flowing,
land is destocked and we pray for rain.

The climate is changing
and we're beginning to suffer.
In wet places rain is falling more often,
saturated hillsides start slipping away,
fields turn to mud and the rivers run high,
land is destocked and we pray for fine weather.

The climate is changing
and we're beginning to suffer.
Temperate climates now have tropical pests,
with no natural predators to keep them in check
they feast on our crops and damage our trees,
in our war with the bugs we pray for success.

The climate is changing
and we're beginning to suffer.
With summers now hotter and winters much harsher
our seasonal rhythms need changing also.
Old ways of doing things could lead to disaster,
in our struggle to adapt we pray for transformation.

The climate is changing
and we're beginning to suffer.
The time is now to make a positive impact.
We can't put off reducing our own contribution
of greenhouse gases with their hot house effect.
We are personally responsible so we pray for insight.

The climate is changing
and we're beginning to suffer;
but the earth is forgiving when we choose to change.
Let us reforest its surface, clean up its rivers,
reduce our reliance on fuels that pollute.
In our quest for survival we pray for transformation.

The Climate is changing
and we must change also,
or face the consequences of our selfish ways.
To rule over earth's living things and resources
means to care and protect, not exploit and destroy.
The climate is changing, we pray for grace. Amen.

# *Solar Sunday*

## The Sun of Righteousness (Opening/Gathering)

*Psalm 119:105; Malachi 4:2; Matthew 13:43; Hebrews 11:16;
Revelation 21:23*

By day the sun shines down upon us
supporting life on earth with warmth and light.
**God, we live in the warmth of your love
and daily we walk in the light of your word.**

By night the sun's rays reflect off the moon
dispelling the darkness when the moon is full.
**God, we daily attempt to more fully reflect you
in all that we say and in all that we do.**

We seek the rising of the Sun of Righteousness
to heal us from the ill effects of our wilfulness.
**God, we thank you daily for Jesus our Saviour,
who says the righteous will shine like the sun.**

We assemble today for the purpose of worship,
to praise the Creator who made the sun's energy.
**We come seeking a city with no need of the sun
for its light is the glory of the most holy God. Amen.**

**Solar Energy** (Thanksgiving)

We are very grateful for the solar energy
that green plants use for photosynthesis.
We depend on this process by which plants turn
water into oxygen and carbon dioxide into glucose.
**Cosmic God we give thanks for the sun's energy.**

We are very grateful for the solar energy
that green plants store as sugars and starches.
These plants are the primary source of our food
and of the biomass that becomes fossil fuel.
**Cosmic God we give thanks for the sun's energy.**

We are very grateful for human technologies
that harvest energy from the sun's radiant light,
like the photovoltaic panels on peoples' rooftops
that feed power into the electricity grid.
**Cosmic God we give thanks for the sun's energy.**

We are very grateful for solar technologies
that give us an alternative to burning fossil fuels,
and mean we don't need more hydro dams that
flood productive land and destroy river eco-systems.
**Cosmic God we give thanks for the sun's energy.**

We are very grateful for electrical engineers
who are developing solar technologies further,
for inventing better panels and recyclable batteries,
and for building inverters transforming DC to AC.
**Cosmic God we give thanks for the sun's energy.**

Our hunger for energy seems insatiable
and our human inventiveness is not always good.
We have brought ourselves to the edge of ruin.
Even solar technologies will likely cause problems.
**Cosmic God we give thanks for the sun's energy.**

We are very grateful for the hope solar energy
gives us of reducing our future carbon emissions.
God we seek your guidance in the development of
technologies that utilise the energy of the sun's rays.
**Cosmic God we give thanks for the sun's energy. Amen.**

## Heat Waves (Confession)

*James 1:9-11; Matthew 6:24*

The sun rises with a scorching heat
and the earth faces another day of distress.
The mercury climbs far higher than normal
and in the fields the grass withers and dies.

God heat waves and droughts are increasing
as we pour greenhouses gasses into the air.
Decades ago scientists began warning about
the dire consequences of climate change.

Forewarned, we were like the Israelites
who ridiculed the prophets you sent to them,
until the armies of their powerful enemies
were at their gates about to break in.

God we ignored the scientists' predictions
and continued to pollute the atmosphere
with the carbon released from coal and oil,
fossil fuelled energy to power our industry.

Now the earth is afflicted with heat waves
and people and other living things are dying.
Yet still we aren't making sufficient changes
to avert the pending climate catastrophe.

God help us wake up to our great stupidity.
We cannot continue to live as we have done.
We belong to those you call the arrogant rich
who in the midst of a busy life wither away.

The earth is on fire in too many places
and water supplies are dwindling away,
the oceans are warming and storms are increasing
and still we fiddle as though little is wrong.

God we have become an idolatrous people
worshipping money rather than worshipping you.
We won't sacrifice our current standard of living
even to preserve a habitable world for our children.

Bring us to repentance, a great course correction.
Help us to understand our role as earth's caretakers.
May future heat waves not arise from the sun's fire,
but from our fiery fervency to halt climate change. Amen.

## As the Sun Rises (Commissioning)

*Matthew 5:43-48; Romans 12:20-21; 1 Timothy 2:4; Mark 11:25; Psalm 113:3*

As the sun rises on the good and the bad
bringing light and warmth to all living things,
do good to both the kind and the unfriendly
bringing hope and gladness to all you encounter.
Seek God's blessings on bothersome people,
for clearly deep down they are very unhappy,
and God desires the same for them as for you.
Be quick to forgive others, always remembering
that God hasn't been tardy in forgiving you.
From the rising of the sun until its setting,
proclaim the gospel of Jesus by your graciousness.
May your praise of God be as fulsome as the sun at its zenith,
and like a dazzling sun may God shine favourably upon you. Amen.

# *Atmosphere Sunday*

**Everything on Earth is to Sing Your Praises** (Opening/Gathering)

*Daniel 7:9-14; Psalm 18:13, 96:11-13, 97:4-9; Matthew 24:30; Genesis 1:2; John 3:8; Acts 2:2*

Ancient One from whom fire flows
and who speaks with the sound of thunder,
all creation is called to proclaim your greatness,
everything on earth is to sing your praises.
**With the lightning flashes and thunder claps**
**we have come to worship you.**

Glorious One in human form
who comes with the clouds of heaven,
all creation is called to proclaim your majesty,
everything on earth is to sing your praises.
**With the clouds within earth's atmosphere**
**we have come to worship you.**

Life breathing One who sweeps powerfully
over the earth like the invisible wind,
all creation is called to proclaim your presence,
everything on earth is to sing your praises.
**With the air when still and when it blows about**
**we have come to worship you. Amen**

**Air Pollution** (Confession)

God, from the earliest days of humanity
when we first discovered the blessing of fire
we have gathered around its glowing embers
enjoying its warmth and its flickering flames.
But by burning wood and coal for home heating
we are releasing deadly pollutants into the air.
By creating smog and releasing greenhouse gases
we are turning a blessing into a curse. **Forgive us.**

God, the invention of the internal combustion engine
fuelled from oil we extract from the ground
gave us greater freedom to travel around
and to go further and faster than we'd gone before.

But by choosing driving over walking and cycling
we are consuming far too much fossil fuel.
By creating smog and releasing greenhouses gases
we are turning a blessing into a curse. **Forgive us.**

God, we have always made tools as aids for living,
implements to harvest food and pots for cooking in,
cloth for clothes and needles for stitching them,
tools to build shelters and the furniture within them.
Now our industry in making an abundance of things
is polluting our air, our land, and our waterways.
By creating smog and releasing greenhouses gases
we are turning a blessing into a curse. **Forgive us.**

God, by us burning wood, coal and oil for energy
we are harming our own health and that of the planet.
We could once more enjoy the benefits of cleaner air,
if we all choose home heating that doesn't burn fossil fuels,
if we all reduce how far we travel by petrol fuelled cars,
if we all buy less and value more what we already have.
We seek your help in changing our polluting behaviours
so that we might be a blessing not a curse on the earth. **Amen.**

## Breathe Deeply (Commissioning)

Breathe deeply the air that God has provided,
and give thanks for the oxygen your body requires.
Breathe deeply the love that God has for creation
and give thanks for the blessings creation supplies.

Breathe deeply the Spirit that swirls around you
and give thanks for the new life the Spirit inspires.
Breathe deeply the hope of salvation through Jesus
and give thanks for the wisdom his teaching endows.

Breathe deeply your holy vocation as guardians
of a sacred planet and its atmosphere.
Breathe deeply a commitment to eliminating pollution
so all things on earth can breathe deeply pure air.

Breathe deeply the grace of God who is merciful
and know that God's love for you never wanes.
Breathe deeply the breath of life freely given
and give thanks for the air all life on earth shares. Amen.

# *Rainbow Sunday*

**The Rainbow** (Opening/Gathering)

When a corrupt civilisation was swept away
and only one family survived the deluge
**in the rainbow they saw God's promise**
**that a new way of living is possible.**

When by our mistakes and our actions
we cause others and ourselves to suffer
**in the rainbow we see God's promise**
**that a new way of living is possible.**

When we are drowning in problems
that seem to never come to an end
**in the rainbow we see God's promise**
**that a new way of living is possible.**

When we gather together to worship
in a world facing a climate catastrophe
**in the rainbow we see God's promise**
**that a new way of living is possible. Amen.**

## In the Colours of the Rainbow (Praise)

*Genesis 9:8-16; Psalm 36:5-9; John 8:12*

In the red and oranges of the dawn sky
God we see your new beginnings for us.
In the yellow of spring flowers like daffodils
God we see the fresh hopes you have for us.
In the colours of the rainbow we see that
the past is behind us and we can start anew.

In the greens of grassy fields and leafy forest trees
God we see the flourishing life you desire for us.
In the blues of covering skies and surrounding seas
God we see the encompassing love you have for us.
In the colours of the rainbow we see that
your Spirit enfolds us and we can start anew.

In the dye extracted from the leaves of indigo plants
God we see the generosity of creation's gifts to us.
In the perfume extracted from lavender flowers
God we smell the sweet fragrance of your care of us.

In the colours of the rainbow we see that
we can live sustainably should we start anew.
God thank you for light with its many wavelengths
that become visible in the colours of the rainbow.
God thank you for the Light of the World you sent
to reveal how to live harmoniously on the earth.
In the colours of the rainbow we see that
we can discard destructive ways and start anew. Amen.

## Creation will be Blessed when we are Transformed (Illumination)

*Genesis 6:5-8; 2 Peter 2:5-9; Mark 16:15; Romans 8:19-22*

God we have a tendency to minimise the violence
in the ancient stories contained within your word,
that warn us that human selfishness causes harm
to all creation and not just to people like ourselves.
In these stories help us hear the urgency of your call
to proclaim to all creation the good news of redemption,
by doing what is right, not merely saying what is good.
God open our minds to the nuances in your word,
and show us how the gospel applies to more than us.
Creation will be blessed when we are transformed
by the words of Scripture read and reflected on today. Amen.

## May Your Life be blessed with Rainbows (Blessing)

*Matthew 28:20; Psalm 37:28; Genesis 9:16-17*

When your life is full of troubles,
when you're battered by fierce storms,
remember Jesus promised to be present
whatever your circumstances are.
May rainbows bring to memory
the assurance given in the psalms,
that the Lord who loves justice
will not forsake his faithful ones.
Remember the rainbow signifies
God's covenant with life on earth,
so be encouraged by the knowledge
of how precious you are to God.
May your life be blessed with rainbows
bringing you hope after storms. Amen.

## The Rainbow Reminds Us (Meditation)

*Genesis 9:8-17; Exodus 19:5-6, 30:16-17; 1 Corinthians 11:23-26;*
*Philippians 2: 5-8; Leviticus 25:1-7; James 1:5*

Covenant making God,
the rainbow reminds us
of your covenant with creation,
when you promised to never again
drown all breathing things on earth.

Covenant making God,
the Sabbath reminds us
of your covenant with Israel,
when you sanctified a people
to be a priestly nation on earth.

Covenant making God,
bread and wine reminds us
of your covenant with the church,
when through the grace of Jesus
you redeemed human life on earth.

Covenant making God,
the rainbow reminds us
of our responsibility to stop
releasing greenhouse gases,
for the sake of life on earth.

Covenant making God,
the Sabbath reminds us
of our responsibility to rest
the land from human activity,
for the sake of life on earth.

Covenant making God,
the bread and wine reminds us
of our responsibility to share
equitably earth's resources,
for the sake of life on earth.

Covenant making God,
who calls us into a partnership
with you to care for creation,
grant us faithfulness and wisdom,
for the sake of life on earth. Amen.

# *Volcano Sunday*

## In the Silence (Opening/Gathering)

*Exodus 19:16-19, 20:18-20; 1 Kings 8:27, 19:11-14; Isaiah 66:1;*
*John 4:20-23*

God who spoke to the Children of Israel
through the smoke and fire of Mt Sinai;
God who spoke to the prophet Elijah,
through the sheer silence of Mt Sinai;
**speak to us gathered together to worship.**

God, if only through erupting volcanoes
could you make us pay attention to you,
we would be like the Children of Israel
**who asked Moses to be your spokesman**
**lest they die when you spoke to them.**

God, Elijah did not find you in the forces
that shatters rocks and splits mountains,
shakes the earth and creates plumes of fire,
**but the prophet found you in the calm**
**after the mountain had ceased erupting.**

God, we don't climb mountains to find you
nor do we build sanctuaries to confine you,
for you are within and beyond your creation.
**You are louder than a thunderous volcano,**
**you are quieter than a hushed holy place.**

God, the Maker and Master of your creation,
we have no words to adequately describe you
or ability to truly perceive your glory and power,
**but you have shown us your grace and mercy**
**so we ask you to bless our worship today. Amen.**

## You Created Volcanoes to be a Blessing (Praise)

*Exodus 19:5-6, 25:8, 29:45-46; 1 Timothy 2:4*

God you created volcanoes to be a blessing
to make available the earth's mineral wealth.
In a cycle of eruption and subduction
earth's mantle both gives and receives.
In the magna of extinct volcanoes
we find gold, silver, copper and lead.
Now we seek much rarer materials
for building the equipment we require
to harvest energy from the sun and the wind.
God you created volcanoes to be a blessing.
Over time the ash spewed out of their vents
breaks down into fertile soils full of minerals,
producing food in such abundance
that ten percent of earth's people cultivate
the one percent of earth's soils that are volcanic.
Great nations have arisen because of volcanoes,
and even the ancient Egyptian civilisation depended
on overflowing river water rich in volcanic sediment.

God you created volcanoes to be a blessing.
We are amazed and grateful for their provision,
while being astonished and afraid of their power.
In giving much they also destroy much,
fields and homes and lives are often lost.
So God while we thank you for volcanoes
we also seek your protection from their ash,
that smothers and destroys all that it falls on,
and from the red hot lava that solidifies into rock.

God you created volcanoes to be a blessing.
With the fire and thunder of an eruption,
you descended on Mount Sinai long ago,
where you made a covenant with a people
you had recently rescued from servitude.
You brought them out of the land of Egypt
so that you might dwell in the midst of them,
and through a descendant of these fearful people
you plan to draw all the world's people to you. Amen.

## A God of Fire and Thunder (Commissioning)

*Hebrews 12:29; Deuteronomy 4:12; Revelation 4:5;*
*Matthew 6:33, 10:29-31; Psalm 46:1-3, 10; Isaiah 40:31*

You worship a God of fire and thunder
but also a God of peace and quiet.
When your lives are full of drama
expect to encounter God amidst the chaos.
When your lives are blessed with tranquillity
listen intently for God's small, gentle voice.
When you think God only notices the loudest
remember God sees every sparrow that falls.
When you fear God has forgotten about you
remember God numbers every hair on your head.
So even when mountains tremble with tumult,
be still and wait patiently on the Lord,
seek above all God's reign and his righteousness,
and you'll receive the strength and deliverance you need. Amen.

# Earthquake / Tsunami Sunday

## As a Tsunami is Overwhelming (Opening/Gathering)

*Jeremiah 7:22; Psalm 23:6, 46:1-4; John 4:14; Mark 16:1-6;*
*Matthew 7:14*

As the water of the tsunami is overwhelming
when the sea breaks the boundaries you set for it,
so God the love you have for us and all creation
sweeps over and around all living things on earth.
**God help us escape the drowning waters of the tsunami**
**and run towards the life giving springs of your eternal love.**

As the wave of the tsunami begins its journey
when slabs of rock on the sea floor move suddenly,
so God human history underwent a seismic shift
when a grave injustice was overcome by resurrection.
**God help us escape the injustice of political expediency**
**and run towards the life giving governance of our Lord.**

As the surge of the tsunami carries before it
the debris of the structures it destroys along its way,
so God the power of evil tends to gather momentum
but your grace is high ground beyond the reach of sin.
**God we gather today as a church of forgiven people,**
**saved by your goodness and mercy running towards us. Amen.**

## You Have Given Us Knowledge (Confession)

It's not the shaking of the land that kills
but the poorly constructed buildings that fall
when they succumb to the earthquake's force,
harming those who work and dwell within their walls.

God you have given us the knowledge
to build in ways that will withstand the shaking,
but we have yet to acquire the wisdom
to house the poor in quake resistant buildings.

It's not the rich who suffer most from earthquakes
even when their priceless possessions shatter,
but it's the poor who own little to be broken
who are left homeless and without a livelihood.

God you have given us the knowledge
to create economies that accumulate vast wealth,
but we have yet to acquire the wisdom
to provide safe homes and secure jobs for everyone.

It's not the strength of the shaking that determines
the impact of an earthquake on a family,
but it's whether the trauma stops with the shaking
or goes on and on nonstop for years and years.

God you have given us the knowledge
to create insurance to mitigate the cost of loss,
but we have yet to acquire the wisdom
to ensure everyone is quickly paid out equitably.

It's not earthquakes that cause the most suffering
but the human inequalities that they expose,
in poor countries death tolls are in the thousands,
while in rich lands far fewer people tend to get hurt.

God you have given us the knowledge
to identify why the poor suffer on the earth,
but we have yet to acquire the wisdom
to share what we have with those who have not.

It's not earthquakes that will bring us to our senses
but the influence of your Spirit and the Gospel of Christ,
when we start taking seriously the teaching of Jesus
to do for others what we would have them do for us. Amen.

## The People Who Provide Aid (Intercession)

God bless the people who provide aid following earthquakes,
especially the rescue teams who risk themselves to save others,
digging through fallen masonry in the hope of finding survivors
when aftershocks could cause broken buildings to fall on them.

God bless the people who provide aid following earthquakes,
especially the aid organisations that provide essential supplies,
like tents to shelter the now homeless and blankets to give warmth,
appropriate clothes, and the food and clean water necessary for life.

God bless the people who provide aid following earthquakes,
especially the medical people who come to tend the injured,
those who work to heal wounds and mend broken bodies
and those who comfort the fearful and the traumatised.

God bless the people who provide aid following earthquakes,
especially those who come to help after the initial emergency,
for like the aftershocks that occur daily for months or years,
the rebuilding of ruined infrastructure takes time to complete.

God bless the people who provide aid following earthquakes.
Help them work with wisdom alongside the local people.
May they bring resources to remote as well as coastal places,
and ensure that those most in need get what they need.

God bless the people who are the victims of an earthquake.
Help them recover from the suffering that they've endured,
and may we not forget them when the aid agencies depart,
and news broadcasts tell of a disaster in some other land. Amen.

## Earthquakes (Meditation)

*Genesis 1:9-13, 24-25; Exodus 19:5-9, 20:18; 25:8; Matthew 28:1-6;*
*Revelation 16:18-20, 21:1-4, 22-26*

Earthquakes along the boundaries of tectonic plates
occurred when islands formed and mountains rose,
and when naked land was clothed with plants
and creatures grazed grasslands and forests glades,
God saw that what had come to be was good.

Earthquakes shook the mountain and surrounding land
when the divine descended to make a covenant
with a people recently released from servitude,
and when they agreed to become a holy nation
God saw that what had come to be was good.

Earthquakes struck the city of Jerusalem
as the morning of the resurrection dawned.
When women came to the empty tomb
and found the entrance stone had rolled away,
God saw that what had come to be was good.

Earthquakes will mark the end of time
when islands vanish and mountains disappear.
When God brings a new sanctuary to a new earth,
to be an eternal home in the midst of humanity,
God will see that what has come to be is good.

# *Flood Sunday*

## The Graciousness of God Overflows (Gathering)

*Psalm 29:10-11; 23:2*

The graciousness of God overflows us
**like a river in flood breeches its banks.**

The blessings of God pour down upon us
**like heavy rain when storm clouds burst.**

The righteousness of God overpowers us
**like a raging torrent in a swollen stream.**

The majesty of God overwhelms us
**like a mighty deluge covering the land.**

We worship the God who reigns forever,
**the Lord who sits enthroned over the flood.**

God rescues us from dangerous waters
**and immerses us in quiet pools of peace. Amen.**

## Flood Stories (Confession)

*Genesis 6:1-7:24, 9:8-17; Matthew 24:37-39; Hebrews 11:7; 2 Peter 2:5*

All over the world ancient people told stories
of devastating floods that destroyed humankind.
All over the world modern people know the terror
of being inundated by dangerous flood waters.
All over the world everyone knows the rainbow
signals the end of the storm and its threat to life.

God, long ago the Hebrew people told the story
of a family of eight spared from a massive flood.
One human alone you found to be righteous,
all others caused destruction and death on earth.
Only Noah, his family, and the animals in the ark
survived the flood that swept the wicked away.

This ancient story contains a stern warning for us,
that flooding occurs when we pursue selfish ways.
We have ignored the warning of scientists telling us
that our polluting activities are heating the world.
When the sea is warmer more water evaporates
making the clouds wetter and rain more on the land.

God we must not be like the people in Noah's day,
who lived as usual until the day the flood came.
Rather help us perceive the times we are living in,
and that we must change radically the way that we live.
Bring us to repentance for the sake of everything living
where catastrophic floods are likely to occur. Amen.

## Comfort those Who Grieve Because of a Flood (Intercession)

We pray for the victims of floods;
for those whose love one has drowned
in swiftly flowing torrents of water they couldn't resist.
**God by the power of your Spirit**
**and through the compassion of people**
**comfort those who grieve**
**the loss of a special person.**

We pray for the victims of floods;
for those whose homes have been inundated
with foul muddy water destroying possessions.
**God by the power of your Spirit**
**and through the generosity of people**
**comfort those who grieve**
**the loss of treasured things.**

We pray for the victims of floods;
for those whose houses have been demolished
by powerful waters carrying off all on their way.
**God by the power of your Spirit**
**and through the hospitality of people**
**comfort those who grieve**
**the loss of a precious home.**

We pray for the victims of floods;
for the farmers whose land has been destroyed
by overflowing rivers that have gouged away land.
**God by the power of your Spirit**
**and through the helpfulness of people**
**comfort those who grieve**
**the loss of productive land.**

We pray for the victims of floods;
for those whose animals have been trapped
in rising flood water with no way to escape.
**God by the power of your Spirit**
**and through the sympathy of people**
**comfort those who grieve**
**the loss of livestock and loved pets.**

We pray for the victims of floods;
for those whose businesses have been harmed
by flood waters damaging plant and spoiling stock.
**God by the power of your Spirit**
**and through the kind-heartedness of people**
**comfort those who grieve**
**the loss of a livelihood.**

We pray for the victims of floods;
for all who continue to struggle with their despair
when the rain stops falling and the water recedes.
**God by the power of your Spirit**
**and in answer to the prayers of your people**
**comfort those who grieve what is no more.**

We pray for the victims of floods.
God we ask that the help they need will be given,
that what can be repaired will be quickly mended,
that what cannot be restored will be replaced,
and that those who mourn a life lost will be supported.
**God comfort those who grieve because of a flood. Amen.**

## Build on Solid Rock (Commissioning)

*Matthew 7:24-27; James 1:5-7; John 8:31-32; Psalm 32:6-7; Genesis 7:7;*
*2 Peter 2:5*

Build your house on solid rock
well above the dry river bed,
so when the flood waters come
you will not be swept away.
Hear the words that Jesus said
and put them into practice,
so you won't be like the foolish man
who built his dwelling on the sand.

Be certain in what you believe
and don't give heed to rumours
that will drive and toss you about
like winds whipping up a stormy sea.
For in Jesus there is the calm certitude
in knowing the truth that sets us free
when we continue to heed his word
and prove ourselves to be disciples.

When in life problems accumulate
like a furious flood rising rapidly,
look to God to help you build an ark
on which to ride the turbulent torrent.
Go out into the world with confidence
that comes from knowing who you are –
people precious in the sight of God,
called to be heralds of righteousness. Amen.

# *Wildfire Sunday*

## God Whose Love for all Creation Burns (Opening/Gathering)

*Deuteronomy 4:24; Hebrews 12:29; Psalm 66:10, 86:15, 119:105;*
*Ezekiel 1:22-28; Revelation 4:5; Exodus 13:21; Proverbs 17:3;*
*1 Corinthians 3:12-15; 1 Peter 4:12; Isaiah 2:5, 43:2, 48:17*

God whose love for all creation burns like a consuming fire,
**in celebration of your compassion we come to worship you.**

God from whom lightning flashes and thunder rolls,
**in praise of your power we come to worship you.**

God who appeared to Israel as a smoky column and a fiery pillar,
**with desire for your direction we come to worship you.**

God who purifies hearts like precious metals in a furnace,
**as recipients of your redemption we come to worship you.**

God who delivers the faithful from their fiery trials,
**with gratitude for your grace we come to worship you.**

God whose words are a source of light and warmth,
**in need of your nurturing we come to worship you. Amen.**

**Our Words** (Confession)

*James 3:5-18; Revelation 3:18; Proverbs 17:3-4; Psalm 33:6, 9*

Our words have the power to cause great harm
like a small spark can set a great forest on fire.
God forgive us when our words are hurtful to others,
forgive us for burning them by passing on gossip.

Our words have the power to cause great harm.
Like a raging wildfire they generate their own wind.
God forgive us when our words spread disinformation,
forgive us when we fan the flames of fake news.

Our words also have the power to do great good
like the burning of a torch brings light in the dark.
God our words can expose the darkness of deception
and bring into the light truth that's being denied.

Our words have the power to produce great worth
like the gold in a crucible when being purified by fire.
God our words can call to account those who support
activities that are warming the earth's atmosphere.

God our world is full of words being published,
words that are factual and words that are false.
God set us on fire with desire for your wisdom
for protecting the world you spoke into being. Amen.

## Wildfires (Intercession)

*Joel 1:19-20*

Every summer, every year all over the earth
wild fires rage and destroy all before them.
More and more precious forest is burnt,
animals are killed by the merciless flames,
homes are destroyed and businesses lost,
as firefighters fail to contain the blaze.

Because the climate is warming
the forest undergrowth is tinder dry,
providing a rich source of fuel for fire,
so that once a spark ignites a flame
it quickly becomes a crackling blaze
that grows into an unstoppable inferno.

God please help the firefighters struggling
to bring dangerous wildfires under control,
keep them safe as they battle the flames,
especially when they're surrounded by fire,
give them rest when they become exhausted,
and success in extinguishing the fires they fight.

God please keep safe the firefighting pilots
who from their planes and helicopters dump
tonnes of water and fire retarding chemicals
to extinguish the inferno on the ground below.
Keep them safe when loading on water and
help them avoid aerial hazards like power lines.

God please comfort the victims of wildfires,
those who have lost all that they own.
Treasures associated with precious memories
destroyed by the all-consuming flames.
Much worse is the loss of precious lives,
loved ones who died because of the fires.

God please guide the veterinarians
striving to heal scorched bush creatures,
the innocent victims of forest fires.
Through the quality of human care
and the efficacy of human medicine
may the pain of wild animals be relieved.

God please help us take climate change seriously
and each do all we can to mitigate its cause,
reducing the emission of greenhouse gases,
in order to save wild places from wildfire.
God please help us to change our wilful ways
that are resulting in devastating wildfires. Amen.

# Part 3: Social Themes

# *Waitangi Day (February)*

**This Land** (Candle lighting)

We light this candle in thanksgiving for this land that nurtures us.
**We seek God's blessing on this land that gives us many blessings.**

We light this candle in thanksgiving for the people of this land.
**We honour the tangata whenua whose tupuna came here first
and respect the tangata tiriti who arrived here long after them.**

We light this candle in thanksgiving for the Treaty of Waitangi.
**We hope to live worthy of our national covenant.**

We light this candle in thanksgiving for the people of faith involved.
**We acknowledge all the signatories who signed in good faith.**

We light this candle in thanksgiving for the reparations made.
**We long that all will enjoy equitably the provisions of this land.**

We light this candle in thanksgiving for God's great love of this land.
**We thank you God for being here among us on this Waitangi Day.
Amen.**

## Covenant Obligations (Confession)

*Exodus 19:5-6, 24:1-8, 32:1-35; Luke 22:14-20; 1 Peter 2:9-10; 1 John 2:15-17, 4:7-12*

God you made a covenant with the Israelites
when they agreed to be your holy people.
Within days of the covenant being ratified
they'd returned to the ways of their old world
and broke their promises by making an idol.
**God we too often fail to live up to the calling
of being a holy people in covenant with you.**

God you made a covenant with the Jesus believers
when you called them to be your holy people.
A covenant ratified through cruel crucifixion
has too often been abandoned when your church
has embraced the corrupting ways of the world.
**God we too often fail to live up to the calling
of being a holy people in covenant with you.**

God you inspired a treaty agreed to by
the Māori chiefs and the British sovereign,
to protect against rapacious colonisation –
a treaty partnership soon utterly betrayed
by the lust for land of the British settlers.
**God we too often fail to live up to the calling
of being a holy people in covenant with you.**

But like the covenant made in the wilderness,
and the covenant you made with the church,
God the treaty crafted by your missionaries,
although broken and neglected has never died
and continues to call us to a new way of living.
**God we too often fail to live up to the calling
of being a holy people in covenant with you.**

We cannot change the tragic history of this land
but we can avoid adding to the injuries done.
By the power of your Spirit and healing grace,
may the many people who call Aotearoa home
live harmoniously together in loving generosity.
**God help us meet the obligations we have under
your covenant and our treaty with one another,
and so live as the holy people you call us to be. Amen.**

## Do Justice, Love Kindness and Walk Humbly with God

(Commissioning)

*Micah 6:8*

The covenant ratified by the crucifixion of the Christ
makes possible our close relationship with Almighty God.
What the Father, Son and Spirit require of every one of us
is to do justice, love kindness and walk humbly with our God

The treaty signed by Māori chiefs and representatives of the crown
makes possible an honourable relationship between Māori and Pākehā.
What the Treaty of Waitangi requires of every one of us
is to do justice, love kindness and walk humbly with each other.

These southern islands have sustained all who've migrated here,
those who came in waka, in sailing ships or recently by plane.
What the land of Aotearoa requires of every one of us
is to do justice, love kindness and walk humbly on the earth.

The gospel that was once well received by the tangata whenua
continues to inspire and bring hope to people of every race.
Go out from here fully embracing the teachings of Jesus Christ
to do justice, love kindness and walking humbly with your God. Amen.

# *Interfaith Harmony Week (February)*

**Many Faith Expressions** (Confession)

God you engage with all people everywhere
through many faith expressions.
Each religious tradition knows of the love
that you have for all humanity.

God you reveal truths about yourself
through many faith expressions.
Learning more about the beliefs of others
helps us to learn more about you.

God you inspire people to worship you
through many faith expressions.
Even folk following the Christian tradition
have differing beliefs and ways of worship.

God you want all people everywhere
to respect each other's faith expressions.
To follow the wisdom of the sages
telling us to live together in harmony.

God you mourn over the harm done
when many faith expressions
became a source of division and strife,
an excuse for us to hurt one another.

God forgive us the evil done in your name
when we despise unfamiliar faith expressions,
when we rise up to crush and destroy
all beliefs that differ from our own. Amen.

**Hands Outstretched in Friendship** (Praise)

God we give you heartfelt thanks
for the leaders of major religious traditions
who are reaching across the divide
with hands outstretched in friendship.
Thank you for the dialogue taking place
between peoples of different beliefs.
May we understand one another better,
and together may we work for peace. Amen.

## Persecuted Because of Their Faith (Intercession)

God there are people who are
being persecuted because of their faith.

There are Christians who meet in secret
keeping their worship hidden from view
for fear that should their faith become known
they would be arrested and physically harmed.
**God deliver the people who are
being persecuted because of their faith.**

There are Jews who gather with courage
in their synagogue on the Sabbath to worship
fearing one day someone with an irrational hatred
will burst through the doors and start murdering them.
**God deliver the people who are
being persecuted because of their faith.**

The followers of Buddha have been maltreated
in authoritarian states and by some Islamists,
and there are Christians who think they're serving Jesus
by harassing Buddhists and vandalising their temples.
**God deliver the people who are
being persecuted because of their faith.**

In various places people of various faiths have forced
Muslims off land where they've lived for generations,
and then they have been denied refugee status
by being branded terrorists because of their faith.
**God deliver the people who are
being persecuted because of their faith.**

There are indigenous peoples who lost
their unique culture and special spirituality
because their ancient beliefs were despised
by the European settlers who subjugated them.
**God deliver the people who are
being persecuted because of their faith.**

God help us to take up the cause of the people
being persecuted for what they deeply believe.
No matter the different names you are known by,
you are the God who loves every human on earth.
**God deliver the people who are
being persecuted because of their faith. Amen.**

# *Race Relations Day (March)*

**Our Common Humanity** (Candle lighting)

God we light this candle seeking goodwill with people not like us.
Whether their skin tones be lighter or darker than ours,
whether their language be the same or different from ours,
**we recognise that we share a common humanity**
**and give thanks for the diversity of people on earth.**

God we light this candle seeking harmony with people not like us.
Whether their customs be simpler or more exacting than ours,
whether their religious beliefs be the same or different from ours,
**we recognise that we share a common humanity**
**and give thanks for the peaceable people on earth.**

God we light this candle seeking friendship with people not like us.
Whether their financial resources be greater or lesser than ours,
whether they have families that are larger or smaller than ours,
**we recognise that we share a common humanity**
**and give thanks for the sociable people on earth.**

God we light this candle seeking greater appreciation
that our racial differences are so inconsequential,
that the people not like us are in reality very much like us,
**and recognising that we share a common humanity**
**we give thanks for the variety of people on earth. Amen.**

## Our Words are Important (Confession)

Our words are important.
They can heal or hurt, be helpful or harmful.
Forgive our racist words, deliberate or thoughtless.
Loving God, teach us to speak only words
that promote peace and harmony.

Our actions are important.
They can mend or tear, build up or pull down.
Forgive our racist actions, deliberate or thoughtless.
Loving Jesus, teach us to act only in ways
that promote happiness and wellbeing.

Our thoughts are important.
They contain secret prejudices, dwell on our racial biases.
Forgive our hidden racism, recognised or denied.
Loving Spirit, teach us to hold fast only to attitudes
that promote kindness and goodwill. Amen.

## Many Races with their Own Cultures (Thanksgiving)

We give grateful thanks for the indigenous Māori people,
whose unique culture makes these lands a very special home.
Thank you for their language, their customs and protocols.
Thank you for their artwork, their dances, and their songs.
**God we thank you for the many races with their own cultures**
**who have come to live in these lands we now call our own.**

We give grateful thanks for the pioneering European people,
who brought the Bible and established the church in this land.
Thank you for their language, their traditions, literature and music.
Thank you for their agriculture, their architecture, and their scholarship.
**God we thank you for the many races with their own cultures**
**who have come to live in these lands we now call our own.**

We give grateful thanks for the Chinese and other peoples from Asia
whose industriousness has brought prosperity to this land.
Thank you for their languages, their studiousness and expertise.
Thank you for the flavours of their foods and their colourful festivals.
**God we thank you for the many races with their own cultures**
**who have come to live in these lands we now call our own.**

We give grateful thanks for the Jewish people who live in this land,
whose ancient wisdom and worship is the foundation of ours.
Thank you for their language, their preservation of scripture.
Thank you for their dedication to you in spite of persecution.
**God we thank you for the many races with their own cultures**
**who have come to live in these lands we now call our own.**

God we give grateful thanks for the Pasifika people who live in this land,
who work hard to support their families here and in the islands.
Thank you for their languages, their dancing and singing.
Thank you for their commitment to you and your church.
**God we thank you for the many races with their own cultures**
**who have come to live in these lands we now call our own.**

God we give grateful thanks for the Middle Eastern people settled here,
who bring with them a new perspective on worshipping you.
Thank you for their languages, and for kindness and alms giving.
Thank you for their science, their medicine, and engineering.
**God we thank you for the many races with their own cultures**
**who have come to live in these lands we now call our own.**

God how much richer we are because of the many peoples
who have travelled from afar to make their home here with us.
**God we thank you for the many races with their own cultures**
**who have come to live in these lands we now call our own. Amen.**

## The Seeds of White Supremacy (Meditation)

Were the seeds of white supremacy
sown when Columbus sailed westward
and instead of old world spices
found lands of new world gold?

They surely sprouted with the plundering
of treasures off the Aztecs and the Incas
by conquistadors whose stolen loot
enriched the Spanish throne.

They grew robustly in America's cotton fields
and in the Caribbean among the sugar cane,
where great fortunes were made by white folk
from the work of slaves kidnapped from Africa.

The seeds of white supremacy
spread around the world in sailing ships
bringing white hegemony with white colonists
to coloured people's lands.

Once proud and independent people
were transformed into an underclass,
and were then decried for failing to thrive
by the people possessing power.

White supremacy prevents white people
recognising how they still benefit
from the wealth their ancestors acquired
from people brown and black.

White supremacy breeds white grievance
over help given to the oppressed.
White grievance begrudges the restitution
of anything indigenous peoples lost.

White supremacy resents refugees
seeking safety in countries considered white.
White supremacy nurtures xenophobia
and leads to the violence of white terrorism.

We white folk who are disciples
of a brown man from the Middle East,
must acknowledge our sordid history
of white racism and in humility repent.

# *Harvest Festival (Autumn)*

### God who Feeds the Birds (Opening/Gathering)
Matthew 6:26-33; Proverbs 9:1-6

God who feeds the birds of the air
though they neither sow nor reap
nor gather into barns sheaves of grain,
**today we acknowledge that you**
**know and supply all our needs too.**

Today we give thanks for the harvest,
for the food brought in from the fields,
the vegetables that grew in our gardens,
**the fruit that was picked in our orchards,**
**and the grapes gathered in off the vines.**

Today the Spirit of Wisdom invites us
to eat her bread of truth and knowledge
and drink her wine of understanding,
**to partake of the feast she has prepared**
**for our life together in the Kingdom of God. Amen.**

### Thanksgiving for the Harvest (Thanksgiving)

Creating and Sustaining God,
we give you thanks for our daily bread;
for the wheat, the barley, the rye, the rice,
for all the grains from which bread is made.

**Creating and Sustaining God,**
**we give you thanks for the Bread of Life;**
**he who came to us so that we may come to you,**
**Jesus, who now lives in us and we in you through him.**

Creating and Sustaining God,
we give thanks for our jams and preserves;
for pip fruits, and stone fruits, and for berries,
for all the fruits from which conserves are made.

**Creating and Sustaining God,**
**We give thanks for the fruit of the Spirit;**
**for love, joy and peace, kindness and generosity,**
**faithfulness, gentleness and moderation.**

Creating and Sustaining God,
we give thanks for our meat and vegetables;
for the produce of our bountiful gardens
and the foods that come from our productive farms.

**Creating and Sustaining God,**
**we give thanks for spiritual sustenance;**
**for learning about you though your scriptures,**
**and for having access to you through our prayers.**

Creating and Sustaining God,
we give thanks for gardeners and farmers;
for the pickers and packers who harvest the crops,
and for the cooks who prepare our food to eat.

**Creating and Sustaining God,**
**we give thanks for preachers and teachers,**
**and all who minister to us in your church,**
**who prepare and deliver spiritual feasts for us.**

Creating and Sustaining God,
you who are Lord of the harvest,
who greatly blesses us with all the food we need
to sustain our bodies and enrich our souls.

**In humility, knowing our dependence upon you,**
**we offer these words of thanksgiving and praise,**
**for the harvest that has now been brought in,**
**from field and orchard, and from your Holy Word. Amen.**

## May You Plant Your Word Within Us (Illumination)
*Galatians 5:22-23; John 10:10*

May you plant your word within us.
May it grow in fertile soil.
May it change our way of thinking.
May it change the way we act.
May it yield a bountiful crop
of the fruit of your Holy Spirit.
When you plant your word within us,
may it lead to abundant life. Amen.

**Everything We Have** (Offering Dedication)

God, everything we have
comes from or grows out of
the earth you created,
and made into a fertile home
to provide the food we need.
We bring our gifts from the gardens
and orchards of the earth,
and the wealth generated
from the resources of the ground.
Bless these gifts for the work
of your church in this community
where you have planted us. Amen.

**For All Who Suffer Food Insecurity** (Intercession)

God you created an abundant earth,
lush with plants to provide seeds and fruits
for creatures large and small to feed upon,
yet there are millions of people in our world
who don't have sufficient food to eat.

Once productive farmland has become wasteland
because of destructive farming practices,
climate catastrophes, and pests and diseases.
Once productive farmland has been destroyed
through industrial processes and urban sprawl.

Communities that once grew sufficient food
to meet the needs of all their families
now find themselves food impoverished,
forced to rely on expensive imported groceries,
often highly processed with low nutritional value.

Even in nations where food is readily available
there are people who are food poor.
People with insufficient funds to buy
the food they need to feed their families,
people whose children go to school hungry.

There are people who can't get access to food
because wars and insurrections are happening.
People are starving where once they lived in peace.
Vegetable gardens can't be tended in places where
bullets are being fired and bombs are being dropped.

God you created a verdant earth.
Help us to understand that our real wealth comes
not from the minerals we scar the earth to extract,
nor from the things we pollute the earth to make,
but from your gifts of good food, clean water, and fresh air.

God you created a bountiful earth.
Help us to start taking better care of it
and better care of the people we share it with.
Let us create a society where everyone is paid sufficient
to adequately feed and provide homes for their families.

God, today we thank you for the harvest.
With hope we pray that all may eat well and rejoice.
With love we bring gifts of produce for those in need,
but what we really want is for human systems to change
so that all people can enjoy the earth's abundance. Amen.

## The Lord of the Harvest (Commissioning)

*Luke 10:2; John 4:35; Matthew 5:6; Psalm 104:14-15; Galatians 5:22-23;
Isaiah 9:3*

The Lord of the harvest says
the grain is ripe for reaping.
The crop to be brought in is plentiful
but few are the labourers to cut
and bundle the stalks into sheaves,
and to thresh out the grain.

The Lord of the harvest calls
you to go out into his fields,
to follow Jesus' example
of generous self-giving,
and as conduits for God's love
to gather in fruits for eternal life.

The Lord of the harvest blesses
those hungry for righteousness,
with both the fruits of the earth
and the fruit of the Holy Spirit.
So go out greatly rejoicing
like Israel in the time of harvest. Amen.

## The Blessing of this Food (Blessing)

God to celebrate harvest festival
we have brought before you today
vegetables from our gardens
and fruits from our trees,
and the produce we have purchased
in supermarkets and green groceries.
We thank you for the blessing
of this food you have given us,
and we ask that it be a blessing
for those we give it to. Amen.

## God the Sower (Meditation)

God is the sower
who scatters seeds of hope,
not just when life is good
and the soil of our souls is fertile,
receptive to God's word,
but when life is full of troubles
and the soil of our souls is choked
by thorns so deeply rooted
they're difficult to weed out.
When we feel hard pressed,
when our feelings are trampled upon
by people oblivious to our pain,
when the soil of our souls is compacted
allowing nothing to penetrate,
God scatters seeds of hope then too
for even here they can germinate.
God is the sower
who doesn't scatter seeds in vain.
Irrespective of the barrenness
of some seasons in our lives,
there will come an abundant harvest.
We will be gathered in.

# *Children's Day (March)*

## A Day Chosen to Celebrate and Cherish Children
(Opening/Gathering)

*Matthew 18:1-4; Mark 10:15-16; Luke 9:46-48; John 1:12; Galatians 3:26; Numbers 6:25-26*

As we gather on a day chosen to celebrate and cherish children,
we recall Jesus saying, "Let the little children come to me."
**God, we ask that our children be always held in your embrace.**

As we gather on a day chosen to celebrate and cherish children,
we recall Jesus saying, "To enter the kingdom be as humble as a child."
**God, we ask that our children be always assured of your grace.**

As we gather on a day chosen to celebrate and cherish children,
we recall Jesus saying, "Whoever welcomes a child in my name
welcomes me."
**God, we ask that our children always find in your church
a welcoming place.**

As we gather on a day chosen to celebrate and cherish children,
we recall that Jesus empowers every believer to become a child of God.
**God, we ask that our children dwell always in the holy light of your face.
Amen.**

## The Children in Our Lives (Thanksgiving)

We thank you God for the wonder of the very young
in the world they're discovering for the first time.
Children inspire us to delight anew in your creation.
**We are thankful for the children in our lives.**

We thank you God for the curiosity of young minds
in why things are the way they are and how they work.
Children inspire us to reconsider what we take for granted.
**We are thankful for the children in our lives.**

We thank you God for the wisdom of children
in their openness to new teaching and trying new things.
Children inspire us to attempt what we haven't done before.
**We are thankful for the children in our lives.**

We thank you God for the imagination of children
in playing at being grown-ups busy at their work.
Children inspire us to find pleasure in the jobs we do.
**We are thankful for the children in our lives.**

We thank you for the depth of faith of young people
in their unquestioning acceptance of the mystical.
Children inspire us to reconnect with the Bible's stories.
**We are thankful for the children in our lives. Amen.**

### Children are a Blessing (Intercession)

Children are a blessing given by you God.
Their birth brings us excitement and joy.
As they grow we take pride in their achievements.
We delight in the sound of children at play.
**Children are a blessing given by you God,**
**may we be a blessing to them.**

We are responsible for nurturing our children,
loving them unconditionally and providing for them,
guiding them and giving them a good education,
allowing them to play and teaching them to work.
**Children are a blessing given by you God,**
**may we be a blessing to them.**

Children have the right to a wholesome family life.
Children have the right to have their basic needs met.
Children have the right to access high-quality schooling.
Children have the right to have fun and enjoy their youth.
**Children are a blessing given by you God,**
**may we be a blessing to them.**

But not all children are welcomed at their birth.
Not all children grow up within loving families.
Not all children are given opportunities to succeed.
Not all children are happy and healthy and having fun.
**Children are a blessing given by you God,**
**may we be a blessing to them.**

Even in our country there are children who aren't thriving.
Even here there are children in abusive situations.
Even here there are children going hungry and cold.
Even here there are children who are angry and afraid.
**Children are a blessing given by you God,**
**may we be a blessing to them.**

May we support young parents to be loving parents.
May we ensure every family is financially secure.
May we freely provide every child with a quality education.
May we create safe places where children can play.
**Children are a blessing given by you God,**
**may we be a blessing to them. Amen.**

## Worship for All Ages (Meditation)

*Mark 10:13-16; Matthew 18:1-5*

Like the disciples we sometimes get in the way
of our children coming to Jesus to be blessed by him.
Jesus delights in our little ones and says that we
who tend to see ourselves as their superiors
must become like young children, humble and trusting,
if we are to be invited into the reign of God.

The church has recognised its error in limiting
the worship opportunities of our younger children,
by sending them out to do supervised activities
while we adults are left to worship Jesus undisturbed.
Clearly there needs to be age appropriate teaching
without excluding children from our communal worship.

So we've invented this thing called All Age Worship
to involve our children in our Sunday morning services.
Our worship should be much more than just child friendly,
for all ages refer to children, teens, adults and the elderly.
This requires a total rethink on how we do church services,
and not just some tweaking of our liturgical practices.

We also have programmes designed to engage our teens,
youth clubs, and Easter camps, and confirmation classes.
It's not that these aren't good they simply aren't enough.
These too can separate teens from worshipping adults.
For the church to be authentic the church must bring
together every age in every stage of faith development.

We actually need a new way of being church together,
which includes a new way of involving our young people.
We need a new excitement about our collective endeavour
to reflect in our daily lives the teachings of Jesus Christ.
We don't need worship to be a sort of holy entertainment.
Rather we hope for worship that is truly transformational.

# *International Women's Day (March)*

### Where Women Feel Supported (Intercession)

God when humans were formed in your image,
you made them to be both male and female,
and you entrusted to both men and women
the task of governing the earth responsibly.

God you did not favour one gender over the other.
We, however, have a long history of doing that,
of giving opportunities to our boys denied to our girls,
of paying our men more because they're men not women.

God we celebrate our high achieving women,
those who have excelled in predominately male professions,
but the fact that they stand out so much from their sisters
points to the career restrictions other women face.

God in Bible times the important men sat at the city gate
while in their dwellings their wives and daughters toiled.
This indoor/outdoor division of tasks often still occurs
even when both partners are employed outside the home.

God, we want to be a community where women feel well supported
in pursuing their dreams and in the choices they make,
when they stay home to be their children's primary carer,
and when they go out to be their family's main provider.

God, women's lives have often been too busy and not easy.
That's still true today as it was in Bible times.
Bless all burdened women, young, middle-aged and old
with people who are willing to lighten their heavy load. Amen.

## Bless Every Woman (Intercession)

God we acknowledge our women high achievers;
the women who are presidents, prime ministers and judges,
and the women in charge of commerce and industry.
We also acknowledge the inspirational mothers and teachers
who are nurturing the next generation of highfliers.

God we thank you for our women scientists and doctors,
for the women who work as lab technicians and nurses,
and for all the women responsible for administration.
We thank you for the women who enhance our culture
through their writings, their performative and visual arts.

God bless every woman whatever her achievements.
May her responsibilities be acknowledged by us all.
During the coronavirus pandemic we discovered that
the least respected jobs were the most important,
done by low paid women deemed to be essential workers.

God bless every woman who supports her daughters
to get the best education they can to achieve their goals.
May our young people find fulfilment in the work that they do.
God bless every woman be she a high achiever in the workforce
or a busy mother who has decided to stay at home. Amen.

## Influential Female Church Leaders (Blessing)

*Acts 9:36-43, 16:11-15, 40, 18:24-26; Romans 16:1-2*

May you be as charitable as Tabitha,
maker of clothes for the poor.
May you be as hospitable as Lydia,
leader of the church in her house.
May you be as scholarly as Priscilla
teacher of the theologian Apollos.
May you be as generous as Phoebe
benefactor of Paul and many others.
May you emulate these early believers,
these influential female church leaders. Amen.

**In Women Like These May You Find Inspiration** (Commissioning)

May you be as courageous as the judge Deborah,
who delivered her people from their oppressors.
May you be as devoted as the Moabite Ruth,
who'd rather leave her own people than leave Naomi.
May you be as resourceful as the Levite Jochebed
who entrusted her son Moses to the care of a princess.
May you be as astute as David's wife Bathsheba
who ensured that her son Solomon succeeded his father.
May you be as insightful as the prophet Huldah,
who was asked to authenticate a book of scripture.
May you be as audacious as the young Queen Esther
who risked her life to expose a plot against her people.
May you be as trusting as the youthful Mary
who accepted the burden of mothering the Messiah.
May you be as faithful as the disciple Mary Magdalene,
apostle to the apostles, the first to see the risen Christ.
In women like these may you find inspiration
for your own faith journey with the challenges it brings.
This day and every day may the God of these women
bless you and keep you safe within her care. Amen.

## Women Leaders in the Church (Meditation)

God we thank you for the women who are serving
in senior leadership roles within the church,
women clergy who pastor congregations
and women with oversight of denominations.

Deborah and Huldah were unique in ancient times,
one being a judge of Israel, the other a respected prophet,
but most of the time the wisdom of women had
little influence on how your people worshipped you.

There are hints of women leading church groups
within their households in New Testament times,
but women were excluded from the public sphere,
and so could not oversee churches outside their homes.

Women started and organised the church's charities,
and established their own monastic communities.
Some were notable scholars in Mediaeval times,
and some began what today we'd call universities.

When Europeans started colonising the world,
women went as missionaries to far distant lands,
but in their own countries women did not stand
in pulpits in their churches explaining your holy word.

This began changing mid-way through last century
when women were ordained ministers of word and sacrament.
The church hasn't descended into confusion and heresy
as some feared would happen should women become clergy.

Women have enriched the church with new perspectives
unveiling the patriarchal point of view of the Bible's stories,
explaining the limitations of some traditional understandings,
revealing how the gospel speaks to modern women.

But the struggle to give women an equal voice in church
is ongoing in hierarchical and conservative denominations.
As in times past there are today women scholars
teaching priests whose ranks they aren't allowed to join.

God we are grateful for all our women church leaders
and ask that their number be substantially increased
by more denominations recognising the authenticity
of Christ calling women to be servant leaders in the church. Amen.

# *ANZAC Day*

**We Light a Candle in Remembrance** (Candle lighting)

**We light a candle in remembrance
of those who have died in war.
We mourn all of the fallen by honouring
the supreme sacrifice they made.**

We remember the suffering of the ANZACS
who died during the First World War,
and mourn the soldiers, sailors and airmen
who died during the Second World War.

**We light a candle in remembrance
of those who have died in war.
We mourn all of the fallen by honouring
the supreme sacrifice they made.**

We remember those who died serving their country
in Korea, Vietnam, and on peace keeping missions,
and the doctors, nurses and medical orderlies
who in trying to save lives lost theirs.

**We light a candle in remembrance
of those who have died in war.
We mourn all of the fallen by honouring
the supreme sacrifice they made.**

We long for an end to all conflicts,
for a time when wars will be no more,
when no more names will be added
to the memorials for those lost through war. Amen.

### Veterans (Intercession)

We pray for the veterans of conflicts,
the young men and women sent to war,
who come home damaged in body and mind,
by what they have seen and had to endure.

We pray for those with life-changing wounds,
that leave them scarred for the rest of their lives,
we particularly pray for those who've lost limbs
and otherwise been injured beyond repair.

We pray that our veterans can quickly access
the medical and counselling support they require,
and that are able to have fulfilling lives,
when their military service is over and done.

We pray for governments to seek peace,
to be slow to send our young people to war,
to seek nonviolent means to overcome evil,
and only engage in conflict as a last resort.

God while we pray for an end to going to war,
we remember those who have been sent to war,
we pray that their sacrifice not be in vain,
that your reign on earth will bring peace to all. Amen.

## ANZAC Day (Commissioning)

*Matthew 5:9*

It is fitting that the anniversary of the
start of a battle that couldn't be won,
is the day on which for over a century
we have mourned the victims of war.

ANZAC Day doesn't celebrate a victory,
but demands that we soberly recall
the suffering, death and destruction
that is the huge cost of the scourge of war.

We pledge to always remember the fallen,
the price paid in lives lost for our freedom,
a freedom hard won and soon threatened
by the next despot keen to start a war.

We might better speak of fighting as failure,
and in remembrance of those killed in wars,
reflect our status as God's children by being
the peacemakers Jesus said would be blessed.

Go from this service soberly remembering
the precious lives slain by bullets and bombs.
Go from this service quietly determining
to honour the lost by nurturing peace. Amen.

## We Remember (Meditation)

We remember...
We remember the naivety of their patriotism,
their willingness to fight for king and country.
We remember that this was not a noble cause,
but imperial powers struggling for supremacy.

We remember...
We remember the greatness of their suffering,
their dying at Gallipoli and in trenches in Europe.
We remember the mourning in our country for the
eighteen thousand whose bodies lie in foreign soil.

We remember...
We remember the sacrifice of our young nation.
From a population of about one million people,
close to one hundred thousand mainly young folk,
soldiers and nurses, sailed away to war.

We remember...
We remember their comrades in arms
from throughout the British Empire,
especially the Australian troops
with whom they formed the ANZACs.

We remember...
We remember the suffering on the other side,
the enemies they called the Huns and Johnny Turks,
who were also fighting for imperial powers,
who were also pawns of unrestrained ambition.

We remember...
We remember the horror and the tragedy
that the First World War unleashed upon humankind.
We remember that the men who sacrificed their all
hoped they were fighting the war to end all wars.

We remember...
We remember the children born to the soldiers who came home,
the next generation who left our nation's peaceful shores
to fight in North Africa, Europe, and close by in the Pacific,
in a global conflict arising out of the first.

We remember...
We remember the ANZACs, and a century later we still mourn.

# *Mothers' Day (May)*

**Blessing on Mothers** (Intercession)

We give thanks for our mothers.
The mothers who laboured to birth us,
the mothers who laboured to raise us,
the mothers who sacrificed much for us,
the mothers who unconditionally love us.
**God we seek your blessing on mothers.**

We give thanks for "other mothers."
The women who become foster mothers,
the women who become step mothers,
the women who are to us like mothers,
the women who unconditionally love us.
**God we seek your blessing on mothers.**

We ask you to bless every mother.
The mothers who parent with partners,
the mothers who parent alone,
the mothers with ample resources,
the mothers who struggle to get by.
**God we seek your blessing on mothers.**

We ask you to bless our grandmothers,
who worked at raising our parents,
who helped our parents raise us,
who love their grandchildren immensely,
who now may need assistance from us.
**God we seek your blessing on grandmothers.**

We ask you to bless mothers everywhere.
May they feel they are valued and loved,
may they receive the support that they need,
may they have enough resources to thrive, and
may they have time to take care of themselves.
**God we seek your blessing on mothers. Amen.**

**Thanks for All Mothering Women** (Thanksgiving)

God we give thanks for the women who raised us;
the mothers who nursed and nurtured us,
the mothers who fed and clothed us,
the mothers who taught and disciplined us,
the mothers who devoted themselves to us.

God we give thanks for the women who inspired us;
the mothers who shared their wisdom with us,
the mothers who taught their skills to us,
the mothers who told wonderful stories to us,
the mothers who introduced Jesus to us.

God we give thanks for the women who supported us;
the mothers whose sacrifices made life good for us,
the mothers whose words instilled confidence in us,
the mothers whose assistance lead to success for us,
the mothers whose integrity was an example for us.

God we give thanks for the women who loved us;
the birth mothers who sought only the best for us,
the foster mothers who took very good care of us,
the step-mothers who warmly welcomed us,
the mothers who gave of themselves for us.

God bless the women who are blessings for children;
those who nurture whether they're mothers or not,
those who instruct whether they're teachers or not,
those who always have time to listen and console.
God we give thanks for all mothering women. Amen.

## Solo Mothers (Intercession)

*Psalm 68:5, 146:9; James 1:27*

The most vulnerable in the ancient world
was the widow with young children to raise.
Among the most vulnerable in the world today
is the mother rearing children on her own.

God you heard the cries of Israel's widows,
now hear the sighs of today's solo mothers,
striving to do the best for their children
with little money and meagre assistance.

God frequently these mothers are judged
for being without a resident male partner.
Often they're assumed to be undeserving
and totally responsible for their poverty.

Jesus you knew the pain of the outcast,
you sought out your community's "sinners."
Lovingly encourage and bless our solo mothers
and help us support them in raising their children.

Produce in us a heart of compassion
for the families lacking the presence of fathers.
Inspire us to hold out our hands in friendship
to the mothers raising children on their own. Amen.

## God Bless the Mothers Among Us (Blessing)

God bless the mothers among us
and those who are like mothers to us.
Bless also their husbands and partners,
and the beloved children here with us.
Together with the singles they all are
valued members of our church family. Amen.

## Our Mothering God (Meditation)

*Deuteronomy 32:18; Hosea 11:3-4; Isaiah 49:15, 66:13;*
*Matthew 23:37-39; Proverbs 9:1-6*

The God that birthed all creation
nurtures all that came into being.
She calls out to her rebellious children
to keep them from harming themselves.
She comforts them when they're hurting
and anoints and bandages their wounds.
She bends down to bathe and to feed them
and with love sweeps them up into her arms.
They run because she taught them to walk,
they sing because she taught them to speak.

She is not without her frustrations
when her children defy her instructions.
In anger she threatens to turn away from them
but in mercy she always turns back.
For she cannot forget the children she nursed,
or fail to have compassion on her young ones.
She seeks to shield her brood like a hen
who gathers her chicks under her wings.
In sorrow she observes their desolation
when they choose to ignore her wisdom
and insist on going their own way.

# *World Press Freedom Day (May)*

### Protect Principled Journalists (Intercession)

*Isaiah 5:20; Matthew 5:11-12, 23:29-35; John 8:31-32*

We pray for the protection of journalists
who hold people in power to account.
All too often corrupt autocratic rulers
seek to keep their iniquities hidden from public view
by silencing the criticism of the honest media.
They ban and banish truth-telling media organisations
and imprison journalists on trumped up charges.

We pray for the protection of journalists,
for those who are being unjustly incarcerated.
We mourn the horrific deaths of journalists
who have been murdered for telling the truth.
We pray that journalists may seek out the facts
and publish their findings without fear of retribution.
Our freedom requires the freedom of the press.

In ancient times the prophets were the truth-tellers,
the people who held people in power to account.
They too risked being imprisoned or murdered
for telling the king truths he did not want to hear.
In contrast the false prophets were the propagandists
who proclaimed good to be evil and called evil good.
Today lies masquerade as truth and truth is called fake news.

Today there are a multitude of apologists for corrupt regimes
and "official" news outlets that spin deceptive stories,
serving leaders who fear losing their power over people
should their duplicity be exposed by the light of truth.
Today a fair and impartial press has never been more important.
God we pray for the brave and principled journalists
taking risks to inform the world of what is happening in the world.
May their lives be protected and their words be respected. Amen.

## Abusive Media (Confession)

God we confess that our delight in salacious stories
has birthed a toxic form of publishing and broadcasting,
that deliberately feeds off people for financial gain.
It delights in the mistakes and misfortunes of the famous
and doesn't hesitate to publish stories that are fabrications.
The vicious criticism of its victims is often unrelenting,
and lives are damaged and reputations are unfairly destroyed.
**God forgive us for having given credence to abusive media.**

As customers of the press we have the power
to discourage the media from abusing its power.
We can decide not to purchase rubbish publications.
We can switch TV channels and change radio stations
and reject social media when propagating fake news.
We can uphold the principles of justice by insisting
that every person in the news be treated with respect.
**God forgive us for having given credence to abusive media.**

Today gossip takes the form of clicking a share button,
and a false story spreads rapidly on the internet.
We pray that we may be discerning hearers and readers
well able to distinguish the deceitful from the factual.
May we hold fast to what's real and act upon it.
May we reject what's false and act against it.
May we be upholders of what is good and what is true.
**God forgive us for having given credence to abusive media. Amen.**

## Conspiracy Theories (Blessing)

God protect you from baseless conspiracy theories
which could cause you to fear what isn't true,
and to make decisions based on false information
that could lead to bad consequences for you.
God grant you an analytical mind able to discern
what is factual and what is cunning fabrication.
God protect you from all who would deceive you.
God bless you with the truth that sets you free. Amen.

# *Disability Sunday (June)*

### In Honour of Disabled People (Candle lighting)

We light this candle in honour of disabled people
who make an extraordinary effort to do ordinary things.
**We light this candle to proclaim that disabled people
are important, valued members of our community.**

We light this candle to remind us able-bodied people
that what's good for disabled people is also good for us.
**We light this candle to acknowledge God treasures
every person whatever their ability and situation in life.**

We light this candle to remind us of our responsibility
to empower those less able-bodied than ourselves.
**We light this candle asking God's blessing on disabled people.
We ask that they know and be strengthened by God's love. Amen.**

### Caring for the Carers (Intercession)

God we must begin taking care of our child carers.
Not the adults who look after children
but the children who are the givers of the care.
The children whose childhood is fast disappearing
as they labour to look after a parent or a sibling.
In families where there is a sick or disabled person,
often every family member is called upon to help,
and the age of the carer can't be a consideration
when the only helper available is a loving child.
God help us identify families with caregiving needs
and freely provide the assistance they clearly require.
Let their young people continue to make a contribution
but also give them time to learn, to play, and to rest.
We must restore to these dedicated young carers
the opportunity to enjoy their fleeting childhood years,
and give them the support they tell us they need.
God we must begin taking care of our child carers. Amen.

## For People with Disabilities (Intercession)

Today God we pray for people with disabilities,
for people who struggle to do what we take for granted.
We ask that they feel valued within our community,
and **that they receive from us all the assistance they need.**

Today God we pray for people with declining eyesight
and for those who cannot see anything at all.
We ask that they be able to move around safely
and **that they receive from us all the assistance they need.**

Today God we pray for people with failing hearing
and for those who have been deaf all their lives.
We ask that they be able to engage in conversation
and **that they receive from us all the assistance they need.**

Today God we pray for people who are without legs
and for the paralysed who are unable to walk.
We ask for them wheelchair friendly environments
and **that they receive from us all the assistance they need.**

Today God we pray for people confined to bed,
for those whose world has been reduced to a room.
We ask that they enjoy human companionship
and **that they receive from us all the assistance they need.**

Today God we pray for people with brain malfunction
for those who can't remember and those who don't understand.
We ask that they be cared for with respect and compassion
and **that they receive from us all the assistance they need.**

Today God we pray for people with disabilities
and for the family and carers they rely upon.
We ask that the community supports the caregivers
and **that they receive from us all the assistance they need.**

Today God we pray for people with disabilities,
each person a unique and precious child of yours.
We ask that they be encouraged by your loving presence
and **that they receive from us all the assistance they need. Amen.**

# Day of the Seafarer (June)

### For All who go Down to the Sea in Ships (Candle lighting)

*Psalm 107:23-32*

We light a candle for all who go down to the sea in ships.
**The candle we light is our prayer that they be kept safe.**

We light a candle for all who are storm tossed at sea.
**The candle we light is our prayer that God will still the waves.**

We light a candle for all who witness the wondrous deeds of God.
**The candle we light is our prayer that they be awe inspired.**

We light a candle for all involved in sailing around the globe.
**The candle we light is our prayer that God will accompany them. Amen.**

### The Men and Women Who Go to Sea (Intercession)

We depend on the men and women who go to sea
to bring to our shores the products of the world, and
to take to distant markets the things we make and grow.
**The whole world economy relies upon seafarers.**

We pray for the protection of those who go to sea,
from the battering winds and swelling waves of severe storms, and
from having their vessels boarded by maritime pirates.
**No ship is unsinkable or impossible to hijack.**

We pray for the welfare of those who go to sea,
that they be well rewarded for the work they do, and
are well treated and respected by everyone on board.
**Intimidation and harassment should be eliminated at sea.**

We pray for those who go to sea and for their families
separated from each other during lengthy voyages, and
often unable to be together for memorable family occasions.
**Every child pays a price when a parent works at sea.**

We pray for the men and women who go to sea
to create great holiday experiences on luxury cruise liners, and
to transport goods in container ships, and to fish from fishing boats.
**We ask that they be blessed for the important work they do. Amen.**

## God be the Captain of Your Ship (Blessing)

God be your navigator during the voyage of your life,
charting your way forward to your desired destination.
In times of stormy weather when the sea is turbulent,
God be the captain of your ship keeping you afloat.
When your momentum is impeded by sickness or events,
God be your engineer repairing your brokenness.
God guide you and protect you as you sail the seas of life
and be your tug boat master piloting you safely into port. Amen.

## The Call (Meditation)

*Luke 5:1-11; Matthew 4:18-22; 19:27-30*

The fishermen were washing their nets having worked
all through the night without catching a fish.
The folk on the shore were surrounding the rabbi
to hear him speak the word of God to them.
After taking refuge in Simon's boat, Jesus asked
the fisherman to row a little way out from the shore.

We too can spend time pursing goals we don't achieve
and when resigned to failure find Jesus has turned up.
He asks us to push our boat out a bit from the shore
and speaks directly to us while he teaches the church.

His teaching completed, the rabbi told the fisherman
to go out further and cast his nets in deeper water.
The great weight of the catch hauled in almost sank
Simon's boat and that of Zebedee his partner.
Awestruck and fearful, Simon fell to his knees
pleading, "Go away from me Lord, for I'm a sinful man."

Jesus is not content to have us simply hear him speaking.
Very soon he requests we go into deeper water with him.
We can feel burdened by the weight of our shortcomings,
and say to God, "Leave me alone Lord, for I am not worthy."

Then Jesus said to Simon, "Don't be afraid.
Leave behind your old life and come follow me."
So with his brother Andrew and Zebedee's sons,
Simon left his family and fishing to become a disciple.
These four were to be the Lord's closest companions
and leaders of a movement that still impacts the world.

Assuring us of his grace, Jesus calms our trepidations
when he calls us to follow him wherever he may lead.
Many are the fishers needed to work on Jesus' vessel.
Wonderful will be the catch when the fishing is done.

# *Refugee and Migrant Sunday (June)*

### We Worship the God of Nations (Opening/Gathering)

We recall that the Patriarch Abraham,
migrated from Chaldea to Canaan.
**Today we worship the God of Abraham,**
**the God of three faith traditions.**

We recall that Naomi's daughter-in-law Ruth,
migrated from Moab to Israel.
**Today we worship the God of Ruth,**
**the God of new beginnings.**

We recall that the Pharisee Saul,
had migrated from Tarsus to Jerusalem.
**Today we worship the God of Paul,**
**the God of amazing grace.**

We recall that the scholar Apollos,
had migrated from Alexandria to Ephesus.
**Today we worship the God of Apollos,**
**the God of teachers and students.**

We think of all who have immigrated
from far distant lands to our nation.
**Today we worship the God of nations,**
**and ask him to bless immigrants. Amen.**

## Like Migrants Entering a Strange Land (Illumination)

God, we are like migrants entering a foreign land
when we open the pages of our Bibles to read
the stories of people who lived millennia ago.
They viewed the cosmos totally differently to us.
They participated in cultures unfamiliar to us.
They were members of civilisations known to us
only through their writings and our archaeology.
In spite of this they share with us experiences
common to people everywhere in every age,
so their stories in the Bible remain relevant for us.
But like foreign travellers in need of local guides,
we also need interpreters to help us understand
all that the scriptures are intending to convey.
So God we come asking you to help us comprehend
the eternal truths contained within the ancient texts
that we will read and reflect upon today. Amen.

## Lament for the Suffering of Refugees (Intercession)

In many communities in many countries,
people are making the hard decision
to leave relatives, friends and homes,
to risk their lives to travel over land and water,
in search of a safe place to live.
**Lord God, we lament over the suffering of refugees.**

Their suffering intolerable, they now flee
wars which they didn't start and want no part of,
persecution for being of their ethnicity or religion,
economic deprivation and sometimes even famine,
and are in search of a safe place to live.
**Lord God, hear our lament over the suffering of refugees.**

They pay their life savings to people smugglers
who promise a safe passage but often deliver death
in overcrowded boats that sink and airless box trucks,
heartlessly exploiting the desperate ones
who are in search of a safe place to live.
**Lord God, hear our lament over the suffering of refugees.**

They are often not wanted in the rich lands they reach.
Bureaucratic processes are deliberately dehumanising.
Incarcerated like criminals, some are separated
from their children, who have come with them
in search of a safe place to live.
**Lord God, hear our lament over the suffering of refugees.**

If they are lucky they may get chosen to settle
in some land far away from the place of their birth,
where the language is foreign, the culture unfamiliar,
and good jobs are often hard to find for those
in search of a safe place to live.
**Lord God, hear our lament over the suffering of refugees.**

Open our hearts to the refugees among us,
whose journey to our land has involved suffering and loss.
In recognising in them our common humanity,
may we warmly welcome and gladly support all who come
in search of a safe place to live.
**Lord God, hear our lament over the suffering of refugees. Amen.**

## For the Refugees Who Live Among Us (Intercession)

We pray for the refugees who live among us,
who came seeking a safe place for themselves and their families,
who came seeking a good place to raise their children,
who came seeking opportunities to work and contribute.

We pray for the refugees who live among us.
May they always feel secure and welcome here with us.
May their children play and learn with our children.
May they enjoy working with us in good paying jobs.

We pray for the refugees who live among us.
May they always feel accepted and never experience racism.
May they see their children healthy and happy and achieving.
May they feel valued citizens within a supportive community.

We pray for the refugees who live among us.
May we always be gracious towards people different to us.
May our children make friends with children different to them.
May we ensure people of all ethnicities are able to prosper.

We pray for the refugees who live among us.
May we delight in the traditions of their various cultures.
May we treasure their children seeing beauty in their colour.
May we be grateful for all the good refugees bring to us. Amen.

### God Bless Refugees (Intercession)

God bless the refugees who seek to make a new life among us.
**May they be warmly welcomed and always feel respected here.**

God bless them with the friendship of kind-hearted supporters
to help them adapt to a new country and a new way of living.
**God bless them with a warm house and all the items required
to turn an empty dwelling place into a well-functioning home.**

God bless them with profitable and meaningful employment,
giving them the dignity of providing for their families adequately.
**God bless the refugees among us by helping us be a blessing to them.
Amen.**

### Welcome the Refugee (Commissioning)

*Genesis 29:13; Exodus 2:15-20; Ruth 2:15-16; Hebrews 11:9-16*

Welcome the refugee
as warmly as Laban greeted Jacob
when Jacob was fleeing
the wrath of his brother Esau.

Be hospitable to the refugee
as graciously as Jethro treated Moses
when Moses was fleeing
the retribution of Pharaoh.

Be supportive of the refugee
as generously as Boaz was to Ruth
when Ruth came from Moab with Naomi
seeking food in a time of need.

Remember you too live
as a stranger in the land,
one who with all the saints
belongs to the kingdom of God.
With the patriarchs and matriarchs
of Israel's founding family,
you too seek that better country
being prepared for us by God.

So go from here knowing
you are loved and blessed by God,
and in turn be loving and a blessing
to the people you encounter
be they native born or stranger. Amen.

### We are One with Them (Meditation)

They have travelled long and far to come to our land,
fleeing greater danger than the perils of the journey
that brought them to our home to live among us here.
They bring with them the wisdom of their ethnicities
and add to our banquets the flavours of their cuisine.
We must give them opportunities to utilise their skills
and not have taxi drivers with post-graduate degrees.
We should endeavour to appreciate their ancient customs
having required them to learn our language and our ways.
For they are now one with us and we are one with them,
and by their presence we are made culturally much richer.
In opening our borders and welcoming in the refugees,
we receive from them much more than we have given them.

**We are All Migrants** (Meditation)

We are all migrants or the descendants of migrants.
We have ancestors who:
crossed the Pacific in ocean going waka,
travelled from Europe in sailing boats,
voyaged in steam or diesel powered vessels,
flew through the sky to get here.

We are all migrants or the descendants of migrants.
We belong to families who:
came seeking a healthier lifestyle,
came looking for job opportunities,
came hoping for adventure and fortune,
came needing a safe place to live.

We are all migrants or the descendants of migrants.
We belong to families who:
were welcomed to this country,
found here a place to stand,
live here safely in peace,
now call this place their own.

We are all migrants or the descendants of migrants.
Some of our ancestors were:
wanderers like Abraham in Canaan
and Israel in the wilderness,
refugees like Moses in Midian
and the Holy Family in Egypt,
deportees like Israel to Assyria
and Judah to Babylon,
immigrants like Jacob in Egypt
and Ruth in Bethlehem.

This land nurtures migrants
and the descendants of migrants.
In this land the stranger should always feel welcome,
the refugee should find a place to be free,
everyone should be valued and civilly treated,
everyone should feel this is where they belong.

We are all migrants or the descendants of migrants.
Whether our families came here in the 14th century,
or arrived after the whalers set up camps on these shores,
they all were once strangers seeking a new homeland,
they all found in this land a good place to live.

# *Bible Month (July)*

## Gratitude for the Bible (Candle lighting)

Just as the flame of the candle we light illuminates the gloom,
**so through your word Holy God you enlighten our understanding.**

The churches have designated this month to be Bible Month.
**During this month we give thanks for access to your holy book
in our language.**

During this month we rejoice in the promises made to us
in your holy book.
**During this month we celebrate the gospel revealed to us
in your holy book.**

During this month we appreciate the wisdom contained
within your holy book.
**During this month we express our gratitude for the Bible,**

and we seek your blessing Gracious God on the scholars,
translators and publishers
who labour to make the Bible available and understandable to us,
**and for the preachers and teachers who explain its meaning to us.
Amen.**

## Happy Are We (Opening/Gathering)

*Psalm 119*

Happy are we who are able to read the words of God
in our own language.
**Loving God, open our eyes to see the wondrous things
in your scriptures.**

Happy are we who treasure deep within us the teachings of God.
**Loving God, your scriptures are our inheritance and the joy
of our hearts.**

Happy are we who live our lives according to the wisdom of
God's instructions.
**Loving God, the unfolding of your words give light and
impart understanding.**

Happy are we who rejoice daily in the hope of the gospel of Jesus Christ.
**Loving God, grant us your steadfast love and the salvation you have
promised. Amen.**

**We Give Thanks for the Bible** (Thanksgiving)

We give thanks for the scriptures
written by many people over many centuries
and then cherished for many centuries more.
We delight in the Bible's stories of beginnings –
of the start of a world, of a family, of a nation, of a church.
We treasure the sagas and histories, the poetry and prophecies,
demonstrating faith, lamenting suffering, conveying hope.
We are grateful for the gospels and for the letters
telling the stories of Jesus, and of the apostles and saints.
**Gracious God today we give thanks for the Bible.**

We give thanks for the scribes
who meticulously copied the Holy Word,
and for the printer of the Gutenberg Bible
and for those who printed the Bibles that followed.
We honour those who gave their lives
to protect and make available the holy text.
We hold in high esteem those who first translated
the sacred words into the words of the people,
and who were persecuted and martyred by a church
who feared these liberating texts in the hands of the masses.
**Gracious God today we give thanks for the authors,**
**the protectors and printers of the Bible.**

We give thanks for the seminary and university scholars
who seek to determine what ancient words mean,
who strive to discern the customs of long ago cultures,
and who dig up the past to discover how people once lived.
We benefit from their endeavours to comprehend fully
the writings of sages and psalmists, prophets and apostles.
We are grateful for the labour of linguists and interpreters
to produce translations to make the Bible accessible to us,
and to write commentaries that help the preachers who wrestle
weekly to uncover timeless truths contained in the text.
**Gracious God today we give thanks for the scholars**
**who help us better understand the Bible.**

We give thanks for the collection of sacred texts called the Bible.
We give thanks for those inspired to inscribe on parchment
what they had discovered through their encounters with God.
We give thanks for those who treasured their writings
and preserved them for us to treasure them too.
We give thanks that for the gospel contained in the Bible,
for the good news that we are beloved of God.
We give thanks for being able to own our own copies
of this life-changing book about our life-giving God.
**Gracious God today we give thanks for the Bible. Amen.**

## Move Our Hearts and Open Our Minds (Illumination)

We know that within the holy texts are eternal truths for us to live by.
The principles contained in the law demand that we live honourably.
The critique of Israel by her prophets expose the inequalities in our land.
The wisdom expounded by the sages is as true today as in ancient times.
The teachings and example of Jesus challenge us to show compassion.
God move our hearts and open our minds as we read the scriptures.
Help us to see more clearly the way of life that you have called us to. Amen.

# *Lay Worship Sunday (August)*

### All Your People (Opening/Gathering)

All your people God have been endowed with talents,
gifts given as a blessing for the community of faith.
From among your people you have raised up individuals
whom you have equipped to pray, preach and make music.
**Today we honour these people, thanking them
for their contribution to the worship of your church.**

All your people God have been endowed with knowledge,
expertise used as a blessing for the community of faith.
From among your people you have raised up individuals
whom you have equipped to be stewards and elders.
**Today we honour these people, thanking them
for their contribution to the oversight of your church.**

All your people God have been endowed with friendliness,
a sociability which is a blessing for the community of faith.
From among your people you have raised up individuals
whom you have equipped to facilitate hospitality.
**Today we honour these people, thanking them
for their contribution to the fellowship of your church.**

All your people God have been endowed with compassion,
kindness that is a blessing for the community of faith.
From among your people you have raised up individuals
who have a heart to serve people less well off than themselves.
**Today we honour these people, thanking them
for their contribution to the philanthropy of your church.**

Today as we gather to worship you God on Lay Worship Sunday,
we acknowledge that the church is indebted to lay people
who freely give of their time and their specialised skills
in support of the work and worship of the church.
**Today we honour every church member, thanking them
for all the sacrifices they have made for your church. Amen.**

**Lay Worship Sunday** (Intercession)

On this day which the church has designated Lay Worship Sunday,
we pray for all those who give of their talents and time to lead worship.
We pray for those who have been trained and ordained for ministry
and for those who combine their life experience with Biblical learning
to lead worship as lay preachers or members of lay worship teams.

We pray that you will inform their study of scripture,
that by speaking to them through your written word,
you will speak to us through their spoken words.
We pray you will inspire their praying, that in leading us in prayer
they say what you wish to hear and what we need to hear.
We pray that you will guide them in creating a worship service,
that honours you by helping us express our gratitude for your grace.

We pray not only for the lay people already leading worship,
but also for those sensing a call to participate in this ministry.
May they receive ample support for such a faith journey,
and opportunities to grow in grace and knowledge.
God send more labourers for the work of your kingdom.
Especially remember the needs of small congregations
and bless those who come among them to lead worship. Amen.

**Blessing on Lay Worship Leaders** (Intercession)

God we gather together weekly to worship
because worshipping together brings us
closer to each other and closer to you.
God we ask for your blessing on the people
who step up to lead us in our worship.
The folk we rely on to lead us in prayer,
the musicians who accompany our singing,
and the people who do the teaching.
Bless all the lay people who step forward
to lead us in worship in the absence of clergy,
who by serving us are a blessing to us. Amen.

## A Priesthood of All Jesus Believers (Commissioning)

*1 Peter 2:4-10; Ephesians 2:19-22*

You are a treasured member of the household of God.
You are a living stone being built into a holy dwelling place,
a new temple of which Christ is the cornerstone.
You belong to God's royal priesthood of all Jesus believers,
called to serve humanity within and beyond the church's walls.
Go from here knowing that God accompanies you
wherever your life journey takes you,
and whatever you choose to do.
Go from here knowing that you will always be
the recipient of God's love and mercy,
and the object of God's joy. Amen.

# *Peace Sunday (August)*

### Remembering All Suffering Persecution (Candle lighting)

We light this candle in the hope of an end to all forms of discrimination.
**We light this candle remembering all suffering persecution.**

We light this candle in the hope of an end to all forms of racism.
**We light this candle remembering all suffering persecution.**

We light this candle in the hope of an end to Islamophobia
and Anti-Semitism.
**We light this candle remembering all suffering persecution.**

We light this candle in the hope of an end to bigotry and prejudice.
**We light this candle remembering God's love for the persecuted.**

### The Peacemakers (Opening/Gathering)

*Matthew 5:8*

Prince of Peace as we gather to worship this Peace Sunday
**we express to you our gratitude for all who work for peace.**

We thank you for the peacemakers within our own families,
who dissipate discord through wise words gently spoken.
**We thank you for the peacemakers within our communities,
who encourage harmony by treating everyone with respect.**

We thank you for the peacemakers within our towns and cities,
who weaken racial bias by honouring cultural diversity.
**We thank you for the peacemakers in our prosperous country,
who lift up the poor and marginalised by reducing inequality.**

We thank you for the peacemakers in our divided world,
who mediate to reduce discord across national boundaries.
**We are truly grateful for all the world's peacemakers,
the blessed ones who will be called the Children of God. Amen.**

## Wars and Rumours of Wars (Confession)

*Mark 10: 41-45, 13:3-8; Luke 21:9-11, 22:24-27; John 17:20-23*

God who foresees,
Jesus warned that human history would be
a tragic story of conflict and suffering.
There would be wars and rumours of wars,
famines, earthquakes and disease epidemics,
exposing the best and worst of human behaviour.
God, we don't have to live this way.
The hideous weapons of modern warfare
didn't need to be made and don't need to be used,
and we'd have enough food and medicines for all
if only we discovered the blessing of sharing.

God who reveals,
the world is full of false messiahs
who deceive the gullible into trusting them.
They promise what they can't deliver,
prosperity, privilege and seductive power,
and serve themselves not those they govern.
God, we don't have to live this way.
Jesus came to reveal you and your way.
He calls us to a life of loving service,
by giving priority to the welfare of others,
and by consistently being generous and kind.

God who forgives,
as we journey along the highways of life
we confess to having often gone astray
by failing to be guided by the teachings of Jesus.
You desire us to make a course correction,
for you want us to travel the path to peace.
God, human history tends to be sorrowful,
but our own life stories are full of your grace.
We praise you for your great love and mercy,
and for the life enhancing example of Jesus,
through whom we are united with you. Amen.

**The Peace that Comes from God** (Commissioning)

*Philippians 4:7*

The peace of mind that comes from God
that frees us from our worries and our fears,
be with you in all the circumstances of your life;
giving you courage to face whatever the future holds
with faith and confidence in the One God –
The Father, Son and Holy Spirit – whose love is unfailing,
and whose faithfulness is everlasting.
Go from here with joyfulness,
and every day live fully in the freedom
that comes from the peace of God
that surpasses all understanding,
which will guard your heart and mind
as you live in union with Christ Jesus. Amen.

# *Youth Sunday (August)*

**On this Youth Sunday** (Opening/Gathering)
*1 Samuel 3:10; 16:18-23; Jeremiah 1:6; 2 Samuel 23:1; Daniel 1:8;*
*John 6:8-14, 35; 1 John 1:14*

God on this Youth Sunday we've heard your call to gather,
**and recall how the child Samuel responded to your voice**
**by saying, "Speak for your servant is listening."**

God on this Youth Sunday we seek to speak your words,
**and recall how the youth Jeremiah confessed,**
**"I do not know how to speak, for I'm only a youth."**

God on this Youth Sunday we make music in praise of you,
**and recall the musical skill of the shepherd boy David**
**who became known as "the sweet psalmist of Israel."**

God on this Youth Sunday we feast on the bread of life,
**and recall how the young Daniel and his companions**
**refused to defile themselves with the food of pagans.**

God on this Youth Sunday we bring our freewill offerings,
**and recall the boy who shared his lunch of bread and fish**
**and the multitude that was fed when Jesus blessed the food.**

God on this Youth Sunday we celebrate our young people
**and recall that when your word abides within them**
**they acquire a strength that lasts longer than youthful vigour.**

God on this Youth Sunday we ask you to bless our worship
**and to bless all the young people who are important to us. Amen.**

## From our Earliest Years We've been Schooled (Illumination)

*2 Timothy 3:14-17*

Like the evangelist Timothy, Paul's youthful protégé,
who had known the sacred texts from childhood,
we also from our earliest years have been schooled
in the great truths contained within the scriptures.
God may the divine inspiration of the Holy Spirit,
that flows through the human words of the Bible,
cause our faith in our Saviour Christ Jesus to grow.
God may we be guided in righteous living
and become better equipped for doing your work,
through the instruction, admonition and correction
recorded for our benefit in your holy book.
God bless our reading and reflecting on scripture
by opening our minds to the wisdom therein,
so that we become more faithful disciples
by being inspired, encouraged and taught. Amen.

## A Magnificent Mission (Intercession)

*1 Samuel 3:1-10; Jeremiah 1:4-6*

Christ who called young men to be your disciples,
call our young people to be your disciples today.
**It is during our youth that we are the most idealistic.**
**Inspire our young people with your demanding ideals.**

It is during our youth that we are the most energetic.
Fill our young people with a drive to be of service.
**It is during our youth that we are the most adventurous.**
**Give our young people an exciting magnificent mission.**

Christ who chose young people to start the church,
choose young people to revive the church today.
**It is during our youth that we are most open to the new.**
**Inspire the church to embrace new youth focused ways.**

It is during our youth that we develop our own identity.
Encourage the church to affirm youthful self-expression.
**It is during our youth that we imagine a bright future.**
**Assist the church nurture optimistic youthful goals.**

God who called us in our youth to worship you,
invite a new generation into a relationship with you.
**Anoint our young people to a prophetic ministry,**
**like that of the boy Samuel and the youthful Jeremiah.**

Help us proclaim the gospel in a relevant new way
to a generation growing up in a post-theistic world.
**Bless our young people with a new vision of you,**
**a transformative revelation, an eternal truth to pursue. Amen.**

## The Young and Young at Heart (Blessing)

God bless our youth with abounding energy to learn.
God bless our seniors with accumulating wisdom to share.
God bless our youth with the devotion of their grandparents.
God bless our seniors with the admiration of their grandchildren.
Whatever your stage in life be filled with the joy of knowing
that God delights in the young and in the young at heart. Amen.

# *Fathers' Day (September)*

## This Fathers' Day (Opening/Gathering)

*John 20:17; 1 John 3:1, 24; 2 Corinthians 1:3; Isaiah 9:6; Psalm 103:13;*
*Matthew 6:9*

We come to worship the God who Jesus said
was his God and our God, his Father and ours.
**This Fathers' Day we revere the God who**
**calls us his children when we abide in him.**

We come to honour the God, who is the
Father of mercies, the God of consolation.
**This Fathers' Day we call upon the God**
**who has a father's compassion for us.**

We come to praise the mighty God, who is our
wonderful counsellor and everlasting Father.
**This Fathers' Day we pray to the God who**
**Jesus called our Father in heaven. Amen.**

## Metaphors (Praise)

*2 Corinthians 1:3; 6:18; Matthew 6:9; 20:25-28; Jeremiah 10:10;*
*1 Timothy 1:17; Psalm 23:1; Isaiah 40:11; Ephesians 6:1; Romans 13:1*

God who designed, initiated and now sustains the universe,
we do not have words by which to accurately describe you.
**We can only speak of you figuratively with words to which**
**we ascribe meaning drawn from our own limited experiences.**

We use metaphors drawn from our knowledge of parenting
when we call you our Father, who is merciful and comforting,
**but our perception of you can be distorted by hard-hearted**
**human fathers who treat their children harshly and hurtfully.**

We use metaphors drawn from our knowledge of governing
when we call you our King who rules over us righteously,
**but our perception of you can be distorted by unprincipled**
**human rulers who serve themselves not those they govern.**

We use metaphors drawn from our knowledge of shepherding
when we call you our Shepherd who leads us to green pastures,
**but our perception of you can be distorted by modern farmers**
**who don't lead their flocks but rather control them with dogs.**

God your role as our Father encompasses many of your roles.
You take care of your family by nurturing your children like a parent.
You take care of your family by overseeing your children like a ruler.
You take care of your family by feeding your children like a shepherd.
God, as children of your family may our love for you as our Father grow.
As citizens of your kingdom may our allegiance to you as our King grow.
As the sheep of your flock may our faith in you as our Shepherd grow;
**then our metaphors for you our God will have real meaning in our lives.**
**Amen.**

### On Fathers' Day (Thanksgiving)

Today we acknowledge the importance of fathers
by celebrating the love they have for their children;
a love shown through the many sacrifices they make,
a love shown through the happy homes they create.
**God, this day we thank you for the men who are fathers.**

Today we express our appreciation of young fathers,
who are learning by doing how to raise children.
We thank them for the fulsome love that they show
and for encouraging their children to give things a go.
**God, this day we thank you for young men who are fathers.**

Today we give thanks for more mature fathers,
who have wisdom to pass onto the next generation.
By trusting and supporting and gently giving guidance
they help young folk transition to adult independence.
**God, this day we thank you for the mature men who are fathers.**

Today we celebrate the lives of elderly fathers,
the beloved grandfathers of their children's children.
They have insights to impart and great stories to tell,
recollections of experiences during a long life lived well.
**God, this day we thank you for the old men who are fathers.**

Today we recognise the contribution of step-fathers
who provide for and take care of another man's children.
They are tasked with raising step-children as if their own,
creating for them a healthy, happy, harmonious home.
**God, this day we thank you for the men who are step-fathers.**

Today we remember the fathers no longer with us,
who live on in the memories of those whom they loved.
Their influence remains in the values they modelled,
the truths they taught and the convictions they held.
**God, this day we thank you for our memories of fathers.**

Today we give you grateful thanks for our own father,
for the positive influence he has had on our lives,
for his love and his kindness, his tears and his laughter,
making the bond unbreakable between us and our father.
**God, this day we thank you for our own father. Amen.**

### May Fathers Receive Support (Intercession)

The world is full of fathers raising children.
Some have the support of a loving partner,
others are tasked with raising children alone,
and some have access on a shared custody basis.
**We pray for fathers who are raising children.**
**May fathers receive the support they need.**

Parenting places a financial burden on fathers.
Some have good jobs and sufficient money,
others work hard but are poorly remunerated,
and some have to get by on a measly benefit.
**We pray for fathers who are raising children.**
**May fathers receive the support they need.**

Most fathers do their best for their children.
Some show wisdom in raising their children,
others are challenged to communicate effectively,
and some need help with troubled young ones.
**We pray for fathers who are raising children.**
**May fathers receive the support they need.**

God the job of raising children is never easy.
Some fathers successfully accomplish this task,
others manage but wish they could do better,
and some really struggle with this responsibility.
**We pray for fathers who are raising children.**
**May fathers receive the support they need.**

God bless all young fathers raising their children.
Help them develop immense patience and endurance.
Give them understanding and a compassionate heart.
Instil in them an unconditional love for their children.
**We pray for fathers who are raising children.**
**May fathers receive the support they need. Amen.**

### The Image of God as Our Father in Heaven (Meditation)

*Isaiah 63:16; Psalm 89:26; John 5:18; 20:17; Matthew 7:9-10*

God we need to rehabilitate the image
of you as our Father on earth and in heaven.
Not the depiction of you as judgmental,
nor as one who appears distant and stern,
who considers only his sons are important,
who is deaf to the voices of daughters.
This image distorts who you truly are
and has been used to repress who we are.

God we need to rehabilitate the image
of you as our Father on earth and in heaven.
Israel's prophets sometimes spoke of you
as Israel's Father and Redeemer from of old,
and Israel's kings claimed you as their Father,
their God and their Rock of Salvation.
But it was Jesus who stressed your status as Father,
his own Father, and the Father of believers in him.

God we need to rehabilitate the image
of you as our Father on earth and in heaven.
As Trinitarians we believe Jesus when he said,
 "I am in the Father and the Father is in me."
All that we know Jesus to be towards us,
loving, forgiving, gentle, caring and kind,
we know are the fatherly characteristics,
of the God who desires good for his children.

God we need to rehabilitate the image
of you as our Father on earth and in heaven.
This image of you has been sullied through
association with human fathers who are abusive.
Our androcentric sacred texts have been used
to justify oppressive patriarchal behaviour.
Human relationships have been greatly damaged,
and women and children have been oppressed.

249

God we need to rehabilitate the image
of you as our Father on earth and in heaven.
You are greater than the limits of our language.
No single metaphor encapsulates all that you are.
The characteristics of a gender can't constrain you.
When we say you are our heavenly Father
we are acknowledging that towards us you are
parent-like in your compassionate nurturing of us.

# Older People's Day (October)

**Against Elder Abuse** (Intercession)

God we pray for the most vulnerable of our elderly,
the people who are totally dependent upon others,
the elders who must trust in the goodness of helpers,
the senior citizens who are most likely to be harmed.

God it is heart breaking to learn of elders being abused;
of the money they worked hard to earn and now need
being stolen by heartless scammers online or over a phone,
or being pilfered by trusted family members and care givers.

God it is heart breaking to learn of elders being abused;
by the people looking after them causing them harm
through physical violence, bullying and verbal abuse,
through over medicating, and deliberate neglect.

God we pray for the most vulnerable of our elderly.
No matter how feeble their bodies have become
or how much their mental acuity has declined,
may we always highly treasure our older folk. Amen

**Grandparents Raising Grandchildren** (Intercession)

We pray for grandparents raising grandchildren,
a responsibility they did not anticipate having.
We recognise that there is great pain in a family
when parents are unable to raise their own children.
We admire grandparents for taking on the task
of nurturing children in their retirement years.

If tragically those children have been orphaned,
then the grandchildren will require comforting
by grieving grandparents needing solace themselves.
We understand that children who are traumatised
can behave badly adding to the stress of their care givers.
We know that raising grandchildren can negatively
impact the health and the wealth of grandparents.

We pray for grandparents raising grandchildren,
asking that they have the strength they need
for the demanding role they have taken on;
asking that they receive the help they need
both in physical assistance and financial aid.
Bless grandparents raising grandchildren, and
bless the children who are in their grandparents' care. Amen.

## When Eyes Grow Dim (Blessing)

When eyes grow dim so that it's not so easy to read
and ears grow deaf so that it's not so easy to hear,
may God bless you by bringing to your remembrance
the Scriptures you have known and cherished since your youth,
that provide assurance of God's unwavering love for you
in all the stages of your life including this one,
a love that will last for all eternity. Amen.

## Looking Back (Meditation)

Lord we first learnt of you as children
when we were brought to church weekly
and instructed in Sunday School.
We heard how Jesus loves
and welcomes children and we wanted
to be like the boy who gave Jesus his lunch to feed a multitude.

Lord we grew in understanding as teens,
attending Bible classes, being part of youth groups
and having fun at Easter Camps.
We were inspired by the courage and trust
of the young David and Daniel
and desired to be strong in faith like them.

Lord as adults we found soul mates,
got married and had children of our own,
teaching them all we had been taught.
We imitated Priscilla and Aquila by sharing food and fellowship
and conveying to each other our insights into your Way.

Lord we are now in our senior years,
looking back over a lifetime of your grace.
We think of Abraham who heard your call
to new adventures in his old age,
and even though we find ourselves slowing down
we are still listening for your call to us to live anew in you. Amen.

## The Golden Light (Meditation)

The golden light of the late afternoon sun
falls upon the red and gold leaves of autumn,
imparting to them a richness of fiery colour
never seen except at this time of year.
God the golden light of your loving presence
falls graciously upon the seniors among us,
imparting to them a richness of wisdom
never achieved before this time of life.

# *World Homeless Day (October)*

## The House of the Lord (Opening/Gathering)

*John 14:2-3; Psalm 19:14, 23:6, 84:4; Exodus 25:8; 1 Kings 8:11;*
*1 Peter 2:5; Ephesians 2:20-22*

Lord shelter us in the dwelling place you have prepared for us.
**In your Father's house there is sufficient room for everyone.**

Lord we delight to dwell in your house throughout our lives.
**Those who reside in your house are blessed with happiness.**

Lord you dwelt among your people in a tent in the wilderness.
**The glory of the Lord filled the house of the Lord in Jerusalem.**

Now you are building a new temple with us as living stones.
**We are being mortared together into a dwelling place for God.**

Lord you are our foundation, the cornerstone of your church.
**We have gathered in this building to worship you in prayer and song.**

Lord help us hearken to the words you will speak to us today.
**May the words we speak in worship be acceptable to you. Amen.**

## The Plight of the Poor (Confession)

*Mark 14:7; Leviticus 25:8-16, 23-35*

God, to thrive all people need clean air and pure water,
nourishing food and healthy homes for shelter,
but what too many people actually have is
badly polluted air and contaminated water,
food devoid of nutrients, and overcrowded shacks.
The slums are packed with desperate people,
while the wealthy reside in leafy suburbs
where the air isn't filthy and the water isn't foul.
They can afford to feast on exotic cuisine and
live in spacious buildings with many rooms to spare.
**Lord we confess that we have benefitted from the**
**polluting processes that impact on the poor.**

Lord you said we would always have the poor among us
and can show kindness to them whenever we wish,
not because you want anyone to be impoverished,
but because you well understand the human proclivity
of amassing vast riches by exploiting the vulnerable.
Our inequitable economic systems are not sacrosanct.
We can change the way we distribute earth's resources
and justly compensate for devastating land acquisitions.
You showed us the way during Israel's Jubilee years when
land lost through debt was to be restored to the homeless.
**Lord we confess that we have benefitted from the**
**exploitation of those whose lands have been taken.**

Lord while in nations far more populated than ours
there are millions of people living in shanties,
we are not without our own homeless people
forced into couch sleeping in crowded dwellings
or rough sleeping in parks and on streets or in cars.
There is an immediate need for more social housing,
at rents that the homeless can actually afford.
Then we need to address the inequities in society
that causes people to be described as working poor,
for poverty does not need to be with us forever.
**Lord we confess that we have benefitted from the**
**economic system that allows housing costs to inflate.**

God forgive us for our blindness to the plight of the homeless,
and our failure to provide the accommodation they need. Amen.

### For Those Who are Homeless (Intercession)

We pray for those who are facing the horror
of not having a home they can call their own.
We pray for those who are forced into sleeping
in their cars or in tents or in doorways on streets.
**God we pray for homes for those who are homeless.**

We pray for those who are difficult to house
because of their addiction to alcohol or drugs,
or because they have mental health issues,
or need ongoing support wherever they live.
**God we pray for homes for those who are homeless.**

We pray for those who find themselves alone
deported back to this land for offending abroad,
who don't have the support of close family nearby
and end up impoverished with nowhere to live.
**God we pray for homes for those who are homeless.**

We pray for those who are helping the homeless,
the organisations that provide emergency shelter,
the people who are building inexpensive housing,
the people restoring dignity to the dispossessed.
**God we pray for homes for those who are homeless.**

We pray for a land where everyone is sheltered
in warm and dry homes where they can thrive.
Help us put an end to the scandal of homelessness.
Housing is an essential, basic human right.
**God we pray for homes for those who are homeless. Amen.**

# Rural Life and International Rural Women's Day (October)

## Country Folk Gathered to Praise and Worship (Opening/Gathering)

*Genesis 2:15; 12:3; John 10:3-4, 11; Luke 4:16; Matthew 13:54-56*

God we read of you putting humans in a garden to learn
to cultivate plants for food and to take care of animals.
**God you have put us in your church to learn
to grow spiritually and to care for one another.**

God we read of your making a covenant to bless the whole earth
through Abraham and his descendants who herded sheep.
**God you have made a covenant to bless the whole earth
through the Shepherd Christ who leads his flock.**

God your Son didn't live comfortably in a sophisticated city
but laboured hard and lived frugally a small rural village.
**God you know the challenges and the blessings
of being a small church serving a rural community.**

God bless the country folk who have set aside this time
to gather as your people to praise and worship you. Amen.

## Well-being of Farming Families (Intercession)

We pray for the farmers who are being impacted
by climate disasters caused by climate change.
Seeing their land swept away by massive flooding,
seeing their land dried up by prolonged drought.
**God we pray for the well-being of farming families.**

We pray for farmers who are being impacted
by competing demands to produce more and pollute less.
Trying to reduce the effects of grazing large herds
by striving to keep land healthy and waterways clean.
**God we pray for the well-being of farming families.**

We pray for the farmers who are being impacted
by economic forces beyond their control.
Seeing interest on loans and other costs rising,
seeing prices for their produce go tumbling down.
**God we pray for the well-being of farming families.**

We pray for the farmers overburdened with worry
as accumulating problems threaten their future.
Feeling that everything is becoming far too difficult,
feeling the absence of the practical support they need.
**God we pray for the well-being of farming families.**

We pray that farmers may be given the assistance
they need to meet the challenges of these times.
May they get help adapting to climate change
and find ways to farm that don't add to its cause.
**God we pray for the well-being of farming families. Amen.**

## Rural Women in Developing Nations (Intercession)

God we honour rural women all over the world
who are engaged in the labour of food production.
Women carrying out the primary task you gave
to humanity to garden and care for the earth.
**God bless rural women in developing nations.**

God we honour rural women all over the world
who labour on land which is not their own.
Women who work hard for many hours every day
and who are often rewarded with minimal pay.
**God bless rural women in developing nations.**

God we honour rural women all over the world
whose success is essential for their nations to flourish.
Women whose entrepreneurial skills need support
to help them grow their own small businesses.
**God bless rural women in developing nations.**

God we honour rural women all over the world
who struggle with poverty and with patriarchy.
Help us to help them become all that they can be
and bless them as they work to feed the world.
**God bless rural women in developing nations. Amen.**

### The Women Who Live in Rural Aotearoa (Intercession)

God bless the women of Aotearoa who live
on farms and rural settlements far from the cities,
the women who work as partners with their spouses
farming the land and producing food for us all.
**God bless the women who live in rural Aotearoa.**

God bless rural women when they are feeling lonely
because of the isolated places where they live.
Grant them opportunities to enjoy the fellowship
of other women who need their company too.
**God bless the women who live in rural Aotearoa.**

God bless rural women who are expecting babies
and find themselves far distant from a midwife.
May the health and well-being of country women
be much better resourced by medical providers.
**God bless the women who live in rural Aotearoa.**

God bless rural women with children to raise,
bussing their young ones very long distances
because of the closure of small rural schools,
or home schooling if there is no other option.
**God bless the women who live in rural Aotearoa.**

God bless rural women who are employed by farmers,
to work in milking sheds and within shearing gangs.
May the contribution they make be highly valued
and may they be well rewarded for the work they do.
**God bless the women who live in rural Aotearoa.**

God bless the rural women who work in orchards
and in the fields where our vegetables are grown.
We depend on these women to care for and harvest
the fresh produce we purchase in our supermarkets.
**God bless the women who live in rural Aotearoa.**

God bless the rural women who are keeping alive
the remnants of country church congregations,
who serve in lay worship teams or as lay preachers
and provide spiritual support for their fellow believers.
**God bless the women who live in rural Aotearoa.**

God bless the rural women in Māori communities
who are treasured leaders among their people,
keeping alive their language and traditional knowledge,
inspiring younger generations to become like them.
**God bless the women who live in rural Aotearoa.**

God bless all rural women in Aotearoa New Zealand
the women who belong to the tangata whenua,
the women whose ancestors came here to farm,
the recent migrant women learning to love the land.
**God bless the women who live in rural Aotearoa. Amen.**

## Thanksgiving for Country Living (Meditation)

We give thanks for the blessings of a rural lifestyle,
for living close to the land and all it supplies.
We give thanks for the soil from which grows the plants
that provide food for our animals and food for us.
We give thanks for lush grass that paints the land green,
for colourful flowers, and for bushes and shrubs,
and even for weeds thriving where nothing else grows.

We give thanks for the water that sustains our living,
for rain when it's needed and for the sun after storms.
For wells supplied by underground aquifers,
for springs gushing up feeding streams that form rivers,
the fresh flowing water the Bible says "lives."
We give thanks for our canals, our pumps and our pipes
bringing water to land when it becomes parched.

We give thanks for the animals we breed, raise and slaughter
who provide us with milk, with meat and fine wool.
We give thanks for the animals who daily assist us,
our dogs and our horses, and our mice catching cats.
We give thanks for our chickens, for geese and for ducks
and for the wild birds that keep insects in check
and greet every dawn with their jubilant song.

We give thanks for tractors and the ploughs towed behind them
and for the mighty machines that harvest the grain.
We give thanks for the machines that cut and bail hay
and assist us store silage in pits in the ground,
food for our herds during the winter to come.
We give thanks for farm bikes and our other farm vehicles
the on and off-roaders that help us get around.

We give thanks and seek blessings on all farmers and fencers,
on shepherds and shearers and upon all shed-hands;
on dairy workers and veterinarians, on pickers and packers,
on auctioneers and truck drivers and equipment suppliers;
on mechanics and contractors, and rural road gangs,
on country school teachers, and country church preachers,
and on all those who dwell in small rural towns.

We give thanks and ask that all will be blessed
whose life and whose livelihood depends on the land.
Bless them with wisdom, grant to them fortitude,
bless them with strength and loving companionship.
Be among them in the country places where they live
that they may be blessed with a knowledge of the One
who commissioned humanity to care for the earth. Amen.

# *Industrial Sunday (October)*

**Work and Rest** (Opening/Gathering)

Ecclesiastes 2:24-25; Genesis 2:15; Exodus 20:8-10; Luke 10:2; 1 Corinthians 3:7-9;
Psalm 127:1-2; Matthew 6:33

It is good to have work and enjoy doing it.
**It is good to rest when the work is done.**

God put the earthling in a garden to tend it.
**God gave Israel a weekly Sabbath of rest.**

It is good to eat, drink, and enjoy our toil.
**God gives us food and the work we enjoy.**

God has called us to labour in mission fields.
**We plant and water but God gives the growth.**

All who are God's are equipped for good work.
**If God is not with us we labour in vain.**

Our needs are met when we put God first.
**We have come to worship the God we serve. Amen.**

**The Sabbath** (Thanksgiving)

*Exodus 20:8-10; 23:12; 34:21; Leviticus 23:3; Nehemiah 13:15-22;*
*Jeremiah 17:21-22; Isaiah 58:13-14; Mark 2:27-28; Luke 13:10-17*

God we thank you for the Sabbath,
the first example of industrial law.
You mandated a weekly day of rest
for the poor as well for as the rich.

God we thank you for the Sabbath,
the first example of religious liberty.
You established a weekly day of worship
for the people as well as for the priests.

God we thank you for the Sabbath,
the first example of animal welfare.
You commanded that beasts of burden
should know relief one day in seven.

God we thank you for the Sabbath
for insisting we take a break from trading,
for telling us to lay our burdens down,
for giving us weekly intervals of delight.

God we thank you for the Sabbath,
for creating it for creation's sake.
As Lord of the Sabbath Jesus revealed
the Sabbath is for healing body and soul.

Restrictions imposed by the Pharisees
distorted the purpose of the Sabbath.
God we thank you for the Sabbath, and
that you made it for us and not us for it. Amen.

### Job Seekers (Intercession)

To be happy and healthy we need meaningful work,
and we need an income that covers our basic needs
for food, for clothing, for a home, and for warmth.
**God we ask you to help all who need to find work.**

To perceive ourselves as valued community members
we need work that contributes to the well-being of others,
and earns enough money to support us and our family.
**God we ask you to help all who need to find work.**

To overcome impediments to finding useful employment,
such as a disability or too few educational achievements,
job seekers need employers willing to give them a chance.
**God we ask you to help all who need to find work.**

To be employable when old skills are no longer needed
those made redundant require retraining opportunities,
along with a willingness to become a trainee once more.
**God we ask you to help all who need to find work.**

To criticise those who have not been able to find work
as though they are solely to blame for their situation,
is the shameful way society shames the unemployed.
**God we ask you to help all who need to find work.**

To be human is to want to be beneficially occupied,
whether a child at school, an employee, or retired,
so everyone needs appropriate work opportunities.
**God we ask you to help all who need to find work. Amen.**

## God Works (Commissioning)

*John 5:17; Numbers 6:24-26*

"My Father is still working and so am I," is how Jesus responded
to criticism for restoring to health a disabled man on the Sabbath.
God constantly works at bringing healing to the world God made,
by working at drawing a diverse people into the Kingdom of God.
God invites you to join with your fellow believers in spreading
the Father's grace, the Spirit's care, and the compassion of Jesus.
As you go back out into your world of work, recreation and rest,
remember you go with the love and the blessing of the One who
gave humans the task of cherishing one another and the earth.
God bless you and keep you and lovingly smile upon you during
your daily and weekly rhythm of work, recreation and rest. Amen.

## New Zealand Labour Day (Meditation)

We remember the Wellington tradesman Samuel Parnell
who in 1840 refused to work more than eight hours a day,
and the resolve of a workers' meeting in October that year
in support of the concept of an eight hour working day.

Parliament established an annual holiday sixty years later,
called Eight-Hour Demonstration Day it became Labour Day.
The working people of this country held parades to celebrate
the equal division of their day into work, recreation and rest.

God we thank you for the pioneers who struggled to get
better working conditions for labourers skilled in their craft.
When if you didn't work Sunday you had no job on Monday,
unionists sought and got a forty-eight hour working week.

We have tended to forget the toil and the trouble it took
to improve the lives of people who depend on daily work.
We've forgotten the benefits of co-operating together
to negotiate better wages and improved working conditions.

Problems will arise when there is an imbalance of strength
and either employers or the employed dictate to the other.
In the past large influential unions have been irresponsible,
but usually it is the workers who are the disempowered.

God we should recapture the significance of Labour Day.
It's not just an opportunity for a long weekend in spring.
It's about honouring the people who have tried to ensure
that working forty hours a week will earn sufficient to live on.

# Elimination of Violence Against Women Day (November)

## For Women Who Suffer Abuse (Intercession)

*Genesis 16:1-15; Numbers 12:1-15; 1 Samuel 18:20;*
*2 Samuel 3:14-16; 6:16-23; 13:1-22*

We remember the women who are like Hagar,
forced into marriages not of their choosing.
Child brides whose wedding is for them a day of sorrow,
the day when their dreams are stolen from them,
their education ended, their potential curtailed.
Young women whose worth lies in their bride price.
Young women seen only as a womb to bear children.
Young women condemned to a life of servitude.
We remember the anguish of women like Hagar.
We pray for all who suffer like Sarah's slave.

We remember the women who are like Tamar
sexually abused by a male family member.
Guilty secrets kept hidden within the family,
leaving the abused to bear the shame and the blame
for the betrayal of a father, an uncle, a brother, a cousin.
Young women being molested by one whom they trusted.
Young women whose innocence is being violated.
Young women being damaged in body and soul.
We remember the anguish of women like Tamar.
We pray for all who suffer like Absalom's sister.

We remember the women who are like Michal
forced to remain in a miserable marriage
by a manipulative man with power to control them.
The love that they felt on the day of their wedding,
destroyed by a husband who loves only himself.
Women who live in fear of aggression.
Women who are told they deserve to be beaten.
Women who are made to feel worthless and useless.
We remember the anguish of women like Michal.
We pray for all who suffer like David's wife.

We remember the women who are like Miriam
denied the recognition they fully deserve,
punished for daring to question male hierarchy,
silenced for raising issues of concern,
confined to subordinate roles by cultural conditioning.
Women in churches which insist on male headship.
Women in churches which deny women a voice.
Women in churches which demand female submission.
We remember the anguish of women like Miriam.
We pray for all who suffer like Moses' sister.

Lord, we remember that you made everyone equal
forming in your holy image man and woman alike,
and that in Jesus you have totally abolished
all racial, and social and gender inequalities
that get used to excuse the abuse of power.
God end the injustice and violence afflicting
women being maltreated by their own families,
women being battered by husbands and partners,
women being marginalised by their own church.
God see the anguish of your victimised daughters.
God hear our prayer for all women who suffer abuse. Amen.

### For the Victims of Domestic Violence (Intercession)

God we pray for the women and children who live in constant fear
of angry outbursts and violence from a member of their household,
families who bear the internal scarring and the outward bruising
of verbal abuse and being often hit and thrown to the ground.

**God where there is strife bring harmony,
where there is harm bring healing,
where there is despair bring hopefulness,
where there is sorrow bring happiness.**

God we pray for the women who seek to escape violent situations.
Abusive partners are loathe to release the abused from their control.
Often this is the most dangerous time for an already battered woman.
Some husbands and partners would rather kill her than let her go free.

**God where there is strife bring harmony,
where there is harm bring healing,
where there is despair bring hopefulness,
where there is sorrow bring happiness.**

God we pray for the families who seek refuge in a safe place to stay.
May they be provided with the emergency shelter that they need.
May they be given the resources they require in order to thrive.
May they create a happy new home in a warm and healthy house.

**God where there is strife bring harmony,**
**where there is harm bring healing,**
**where there is despair bring hopefulness,**
**where there is sorrow bring happiness.**

God we pray for the perpetrators of domestic violence,
who themselves may have been abused when growing up.
God help them break the tragic cycle of family dysfunction
by moving them to seek the help they need in order to change.

**God where there is strife bring harmony,**
**where there is harm bring healing,**
**where there is despair bring hopefulness,**
**where there is sorrow bring happiness.**

May we bring about a society in which all women live free
from the fear that comes when they are bullied and abused.
May we bring about a society in which all people are free
by everyone being valued, respected, supported and loved. Amen.

## Harassment of Girls (Intercession)

God we want our teenagers to be happy,
to develop their own sense of identity,
to achieve their demanding educational goals,
and to safely socialise with friends of both genders.

God we have become a society in which
sexual activity is often detached from love,
and pornography is now so readily available
that it distorts the thinking of teenage boys.

Sexual harassment of girls is occurring,
and this is becoming normalised behaviour
among our adolescents who don't understand
that a healthy relationship requires respect.

God for the sake of our girls and our boys
we need to develop a responsible society
in which outgoing concern for one another
determines each person's sexual behaviour.

By changing our entertainment and on-line content,
as much as through new educational programmes,
may our culture undergo a major correction
that leads to a decline in sexual harassment.

God, forgive us for all that we have contributed
to the harm being done to our emerging women,
and help us suppress the disgraceful behaviour
of the negative influencers of our teenage boys. Amen.

# World Day against Trafficking in Persons (July) and International Day for Abolishing Modern Slavery (December)

## For the Victims of Traffickers (Candle lighting)

*Genesis 37:12-36; Exodus 3:1-12*

We light this candle for all the people
who have become victims of traffickers,
**like Joseph who was sold by his brothers**
**to Midianites who then sold him to Potiphar.**

We light this candle in the hope that
trafficked persons will regain their freedom,
**like the Israelites who were delivered by God**
**from the bondage they endured in ancient Egypt. Amen.**

## Child Slavery (Intercession)

God we ask for the end of extreme poverty
that leads to parents selling their children,
and we pray for the end of human trafficking
enslaving the world's most vulnerable people.

God may the earth's abundant resources
be more equitably distributed on the earth,
so a family is not driven by hunger and debt
to betray a young person they should protect.

God we ask for the end of sexual exploitation
of young girls who are forced into prostitution,
and for an end to adolescent girls being made
to marry older men who have purchased them.

God may children not be compelled to work
in dangerous situations in poorly run factories,
and sent into the fields to labour long in the sun,
and be in danger of drowning when forced to fish.

God we ask for the end of the kidnapping of boys
who are forced to become child soldiers,
by militias who are engaged in tribal wars
and terrorists bombing their way into power.

God may a good education be the birthright
of every young person irrespective of gender,
so that every girl and every boy can accomplish
all that their abilities and hard work can achieve.

God we ask that governments be empowered
to stamp out human trafficking and abolish slavery,
and that some of the wealth of the very rich
be used to support the children of the very poor. Amen.

### The Abolition of Modern Slavery (Intercession)

May our shops be filled by ethically sourced products,
rather than cheap imported items made by people
who are forced to labour without pay for their work.
**God help bring about the abolition of modern slavery.**

May our industries be required to source materials
and components from suppliers who are ethical,
who treat their workers well and pay them adequately.
**God help bring about the abolition of modern slavery.**

May our agricultural products be harvested ethically
when seasonal workers are brought in from overseas.
May all their needs be meet and may they be paid generously.
**God help bring about the abolition of modern slavery.**

May we be a people who care more for other people
than for the things and the wealth their labour generates.
May we work for all people to have a good quality of life.
**God help bring about the abolition of modern slavery.**

May each of us do our part to combat this modern evil,
by the power of our purse and by our political voice.
While alone we are impotent, together we are strong.
**God help bring about the abolition of modern slavery. Amen.**

## Hear the Crying of the People in Bondage (Intercession)

*Exodus 3:7-10*

Forty million people in some form of slavery.
Forty million people an inconceivable number.
Eight times the population of our blessed land.
Forty million people living in misery.
**Lord God, hear the crying of the people in bondage.**
**Hear as you heard the Israelites in Egypt long ago.**

Thirty million people in bonded labour.
Thirty million exploited in Asia and the Pacific,
producing goods for us to buy cheaply in our land.
Thirty million people working in misery.
**Lord God, hear the crying of the people in bondage**
**Hear as you heard the Israelites in Egypt long ago.**

Ten million children being exploited for money.
Ten million children being robbed of their childhood,
not getting the schooling they want and deserve.
Ten million children toiling in misery.
**Lord God, hear the crying of the children in bondage**
**Hear us as you heard the Israelites in Egypt long ago.**

Five million people being sexually exploited,
most of them vulnerable women and girls,
among their abusers people from our land.
Five million people trafficked into misery.
**Lord God, hear the crying of those in sexual slavery.**
**Hear as you heard the Israelites in Egypt long ago.**

Four million people enslaved by their governments.
Four million people betrayed by their leaders,
subject to the cruelty of brutal regimes.
Four million people imprisoned in misery.
**Lord God, hear the crying of the people in bondage**
**Hear us as you heard the Israelites in Egypt long ago.**

God these statistics are horrific to contemplate.
How can we abolish this evil for good?
Show us how to end the heartless exploitation of
forty million people trapped in misery.
**Lord God, hear our crying for the people in bondage**
**Hear us as you heard the Israelites in Egypt long ago.**

Raise up for us leaders like Moses and Aaron
and have them confront the corrupt people in power,
who profit from the enslavement of so many people,
the powerless oppressed crying out in misery.
**Lord God, hear our crying for the people in bondage.**
**Hear us as you heard the Israelites in Egypt long ago.**

Bring liberation to those in servitude in Africa,
in the Americas, in Asia and in the Pacific.
Help each of us commit to doing what we can
to deliver people from the misery of slavery.
**Lord God, hear our crying for the people in bondage.**
**Hear us as you heard the Israelites in Egypt long ago. Amen.**

# *International Universal Health Coverage Day (December)*

**Healing Lord** (Praise/Confession)

Lamentations 3:22-23; Psalm 103:1-5; John 8:31-32

Healing Lord, we thank you
for your mercy and steadfast love,
and we don't forget your many blessings,
your willingness to forgive our faults,
and to heal us of our many diseases.

Healing Lord, we thank you
for inspiring scientists to do research
into the causes and cures of diseases,
for the blessing of modern medicine
and the skill of medical professionals.

Healing Lord, we remember
that beginning with the first significant cities
and the trade occurring between them,
there have been plagues and epidemics
as viruses have been taken from place to place.

Healing Lord, we thank you
for the vaccines we now have that can restrict
the spread of deadly diseases among us,
and drugs that have proved effective
in minimising the severity of infections.

Healing Lord, we acknowledge
what we haven't achieved and must do
to make these therapeutics readily available
to everyone everywhere in the world,
so that the poor like the rich can be made well.

Healing Lord, we acknowledge
we need to repent of our corporate greed,
racial prejudice, corruption and other barriers,
that restrict poorer nations from accessing
the drugs that could help their people survive.

Healing Lord, we acknowledge
there is another epidemic that afflicts us,
the spread of misinformation and lies,
that deceive people into being afraid
of the vaccines that could keep them well.

Healing Lord, we remember
that you said that if we continued in your word
we'd know the truth that would make us free,
free to uncover the mysteries of new viruses,
free to find ways of providing vaccines to all. Amen.

## Health Coverage for All (Intercession)

God we give grateful thanks that the universe
is a creation that operates according to law,
which makes possible the scientific enquiry
that is the foundation of modern medicine.

God we give grateful thanks for the research
undertaken to discover the cause of disease,
and for the development of drugs that help
restore to health people who are unwell.

God we are grateful for the efficacy of vaccines
in limiting the spread of deadly viruses,
and for those who selflessly nurse the sick
when no prevention or effective cure exists.

God we are grateful for our access to health care
which is readily available and largely affordable,
and we pray for those for whom distance and cost
are barriers to getting the medical help they need.

God we seek health coverage for everyone
no matter who they are or where they reside,
so that even the most impoverished family
can get medical assistance when someone is sick.

God we seek universal health coverage,
so that effective treatments and medicines,
that enhance the quality of life of the unwell,
aren't limited to people who live in rich lands.

God we are grateful for the call that is being made
for wealthy nations to share their medical resources
with the less well-off countries of the world,
so there'll be health coverage available for all. Amen.

# Suggested Readings for Special Observances

Unless otherwise indicated, these readings are suggestions made by the author and are not obligatory. Readers may select other scriptures or use the readings listed in a lectionary they use.

| Theme | First Reading | Psalm | Second Reading | Gospel |
|---|---|---|---|---|
| New Year* | Eccl. 3:1-15 | Ps. 8 | Rev. 21:1-6a | Mt. 25:31-46 |
| Waitangi Day* | Deut. 10:12-21 | Ps. 144:9-15 | 1 Cor. 1:26-31 | Mt. 6:19-24 |
| Interfaith Harmony | Gen. 33:1-15 | Ps. 67 | 1 Jn. 4:16b-21 | Mt. 15:21-28 |
| Race Relations | Exod. 2:11-22 | Ps. 133 | Eph. 4:25-5:1 | Jn. 4:4-26 |
| Children's Day | 1 Sam. 1-19 | Ps. 128 | 1 Jn. 2:7-17 | Lk. 18:15-17 |
| International Women's Day | Prov. 9:1-6 | Ps. 113 | Acts 18:24-28 | Lk. 10:38-42 |
| Harvest Thanksgiving* | Deut. 26:1-11 | Ps. 126 | Gal. 6:6-10 | Mt. 13:1-13, 18-23 |
| ANZAC Day* | Isa. 52:7-12 | Ps. 76 | Eph. 6:1-20 | Lk. 6:27-36 |
| Mothers' Day* | Isa. 6:10-13 | Ps. 84:1-4 | 1 Jn. 4:7-12, 20-21 | Lk. 2:40-52 |
| Christian Unity | Acts 4:32-35 | Ps. 133:1-3 | Eph. 4:1-5, 11-13 | Jn. 15:1-17 |
| Day of the Seafarer | Jonah 1:1-17 or 1 Kgs. 9:26-28 | Ps. 107:23-32 | Acts 27:9-26, 39-44 | Lk. 8:22-25 |
| Refugee & Migrant Sunday | Gn. 27:41-28:5 or Gen. 12:1-8 | Ps. 12-24 or Ps. 105:7-15 | Rom. 13:8-10 or Heb. 11:8-16 | Lk. 10:25-37 or Mt. 8:5-13 |
| Press Freedom Day | 2 Chron. 18:1-27 | Ps 64 | Jam. 3:1-12 | Mt. 10:26-32 |
| Disability Sunday | Isa. 35:1-7 | Ps. 146 | Acts 3:1-10 | Lk. 5:17-26 |
| Bible Month | 2 Kgs. 22:3-16 | Ps. 119:97-104 | 2 Tim. 3:14-17 | Mt. 5:17-20 |
| Peace Sunday* | Micah 4:1-4 | Ps. 85 | 2 Cor. 5:16-20 | Jn. 20:19-21 or Mt. 5:1-12 |
| Lay Worship Sunday | Neh. 8:1-3 | Ps. 52:8-9 | Eph. 4:11-16 | Jn. 16:12-15 |
| Youth Sunday | Jer. 1:4-10 | Ps. 25:4-10 | 1 Tim. 4:6-16 | Mt. 19:16-22 |
| Fathers' Day* | Gen. 37:19-24, 29-35 | Ps. 103:6-13 | Eph. 6:1-4 | Mt. 1:18-25 |

| Spring/Flower Festival | Gen. 1:1-5, 11-13 | Ps. 104 | 1 Cor. 3:1-9 | Mt. 13:24-30 |
|---|---|---|---|---|
| Creation Day | Gen. 1 – 2:4 | Ps. 148:1-14 | Col. 1:15-19 | Jn. 1:1-4, 10-13 |
| St Francis of Assisi Day: Blessing of the Animals | Job 39:1-30 or Gen. 2:18-25 | Ps. 104:14-24 | 1 Pet. 5:1-7 | Lk. 15:1-7 |
| Older People's Day | Gen. 27:1-29 | Ps. 72:17-21 | 1 Tim. 5:1-8 | Lk. 7:11-17 |
| World Homeless Day | Isa. 58:6-10 | Ps. 84:1-12 | Jam. 2:14-26 | Lk. 8:26-39 |
| Industrial Sunday | Eccl. 3:9-15 | Ps. 127:1-2 | 1 Cor. 3:5-15 | Mt. 6:25-33 |
| Elimination of Violence Against Women | 2 Sam. 13:1-22 or Jg. 11:29-40 | Ps. 71:1-6 | Eph. 5:25-33 | Jn. 8:1-10 |
| Rural Life | Amos 9:13-15 | Ps. 107:35-43 | Gal. 6:7-10 | Mt. 13:24-30 |
| Human Trafficking and Modern Slavery | Gen. 37:12-36 or Ex. 5:1-18 | Ps.105:16-22 | Gal. 3:28-29 | Lk. 12:35-48 |
| Universal Health Coverage Day | 2 Kgs. 20:1-7 | Ps. 41:1-3 | Acts 28:1-10 | Lk. 10:25-37 |

*Readings for these days are those specified as "additional readings" in the Lectionary and Calendar published in New Zealand annually by the Methodist Faith and Order Committee: https://www.methodist.org.nz/whakapono/orders-of-services/lectionary/

# Suggested Readings for Season of Creation

| Theme | First Reading | Psalm | Second Reading | Gospel |
|---|---|---|---|---|
| **Year A: The Spirit Series** The Spirit breathes life into creation, suffers with creation, and renews all creation | | | | |
| **Forest Sunday** | Gen. 2:4b-22 | Ps. 139:13-16 | Acts 17:22-28 | Jn. 3:1-16 |
| **Land Sunday** | Gen. 3:14-19; 4:8-16 | Ps. 139:7-12 | Rom. 5:12-17 | Mt. 12:38-40 |
| **Wilderness Sunday** | Joel 1:8-10, 17-20 | Ps. 18:6-19 | Rom. 8:18-27 | Mt. 3:13-4:2 |
| **River Sunday** | Gen. 8:20-22; 9:12-17 | Ps. 104:27-33 | Rev. 22:1-5 | Mt. 28:1-10 |
| **Year B: The Word Series** The Word summons forth creation, evokes praise of creation and stirs life in creation | | | | |
| **Planet Earth Sunday** | Gen. 1:1-25 | Ps. 33:1-9 | Rom. 1:18-23 | Jn. 1:1-14 |
| **Humanity Sunday** | Gen. 1:26-28 | Ps. 8 | Phil. 1:1-8 | Mk. 10:41-45 |
| **Sky Sunday** | Jer. 4:23-28 | Ps. 19:1-6 | Phil. 2:14-18 | Mk. 15:33-39 |
| **Mountain Sunday** | Isa. 65:17-25 | Ps. 48:1-11 | Rom. 8:28-39 | Mk. 16:14-18 |
| **Year C: The Wisdom Series** Wisdom designs creation and enables the roles of each part of creation to be fulfilled | | | | |
| **Ocean Sunday** | Job 38:1-18 | Ps. 104:1-9, 24-26 | Eph. 1:3-10 | Lk. 5:1-11 |
| **Fauna Sunday** | Job 39:1-8, 26-30 | Ps. 104:14-23 | 1 Cor. 1:10-23 | Lk. 12:22-31 |
| **Storm Sunday** | Job 28:20-27 | Ps. 29 | 1 Cor. 1:21-31 | Lk. 8:22-25 |
| **Cosmos Sunday** | Pro. 8:22-31 | Ps. 148 | Col. 1:15-20 | Jn. 6:41-51 |

| Climate Change Series | | | | |
|---|---|---|---|---|
| **Climate Sunday** | Job 28:22-23 | Ps. 104:1-13 | Jam. 3:13-18 | Mt. 16:1-4 |
| **Solar Sunday** | Gen. 1:14-16 | Ps. 19:1-6 | Col. 1:15-20 | Mt. 5:43-48 |
| **Atmosphere Sunday** | Gen. 2:4b-9 | Ps. 104:27-30 | Rom. 8:26-28 | Jn. 3:1-10 |
| **Rainbow Sunday** | Gen. 9:8-17 | Ps. 33:4-9 | 1 Cor. 11:13-26 | Mk. 16:14-15 |

| Natural Disasters Series | | | | |
|---|---|---|---|---|
| **Volcano Sunday** | Exod. 19:16-23 | Ps. 104:31-35 | 1 Cor. 2:1-10 | Mt. 17:1-8 |
| **Earthquake/ Tsunami Sunday** | Hab. 3:1-6, 17-19 | Ps. 68:1-10 | Eph. 1:15-22 | Mt. 27:45-55 |
| **Flood Sunday** | Gen. 6:5-22 | Ps. 93 | Heb. 11:1-16 or Jam. 1:22-27 | Lk. 6:46-49 |
| **Wildfire Sunday** | 1 Kgs. 19:1-14 | Ps. 29 | Acts 2:1-15 | Mt. 3:1-12 |

For information about the Season of Creation, including readings and liturgies, see the website maintained by the Uniting Church of Australia: https://seasonofcreation.com

# *Scripture Index*

# About the Author

Childhood influences have significantly shaped Joy's life. She spent her childhood and teen years on a small dairy farm in Korere Valley, at the mid-way point between Nelson city and Murchison on State Highway 6. Although during this phase of their lives, her parents weren't regular church goers, they were people of faith. Her father, in particular, was deeply spiritual and profoundly connected to the land he farmed and the animals on it. He successfully grew crops according to the principles of organic agriculture, which in the 1960s was considered an eccentric and uneconomical method of farming.

There were small pockets of native bush on the farm to provide a home for native birds like kererū, tui, korimako, pīwakawaka, and miromiro. Nights were disturbed by the "more pork" call of the ruru. Joy grew up with an appreciation for the natural world, which she captures in her Season of Creation prayers. Concern for the world and its people was often expressed in the Kingsbury household, and this influence finds expression many decades later in Joy's prayers on humanitarian issues.

A few years after graduating from the University of Canterbury, where Joy had studied English language and literature and classics, she began working for the Christchurch City Council, a career that would last thirty one years. She initially worked on environmental health projects, and later found immense satisfaction working in road safety and school travel planning, as would be expected of someone with a keen awareness of environmental and social justice issues.

Almost two decades after graduating from the University of Canterbury, Joy returned to university studies, this time to study part-time for the Bachelor of Theology degree through the University of Otago's distance learning programme, majoring in Biblical Studies with a minor in Pastoral Theology. By limiting herself to a manageable one paper per semester, while in full-time employment, Joy committed herself to a lengthy period of study.

Following graduation, Joy's adventure into lay preaching began, which has involved not just leading worship for Presbyterian, Methodist and Uniting churches in Christchurch, but helping provide liturgical resources for other lay preachers through the activities of local and national committees of lay preachers, such as the New Zealand Lay Preachers Association, for which Joy served as President for several years. Joy has been sharing her creativity with fellow worship leaders for many years, and is delighted when she learns of specific occasions when her writings have been used to support worship. *Prayers for Southern People* is a companion book to *Prayers for Southern Seasons*, which was published in 2019.

Joy is now retired, and lives in Christchurch with her husband David, without whose support her lay preaching ministry could not occur. She attends the Village Presbyterian Church in Bryndwr.

• • •

## Also by Joy Kingsbury-Aitken and published by Philip Garside Publishing Ltd

### Prayers for Southern Seasons:
*Poems and prayers for Christian worship and devotions*
Published: May 2019

B/W text, 122pp. Soft cover

**Print books and eBooks available**

Worship leaders, this engaging collection of prayers will support your work of creating meaningful services that reflect the church year in our part of the world.

In Aotearoa New Zealand the church year begins in early summer, harvest comes during the fast of Lent, and we celebrate Easter not when life is emerging anew in a burst of spring flowering but when leaves are turning red and gold and falling to the ground. The prayers and poems in this collection have been arranged to reflect the cycle of the seasons as we experience them, and the church's feasts and fasts, and other commemorations, as they occur within those seasons.

Joy's hope is that this book will be a useful resource for worship leaders, providing just the right words when they need them, and that they, and others who happen to open these pages, may find within sparks of inspiration to ignite their own devotional creativity.

www.ingramcontent.com/pod-product-compliance
Lightning Source LLC
Chambersburg PA
CBHW070911120626

46546CB00001B/225